MURDER & CRIME

BIRMINGHAM

Vanessa Morgan

The
History
Press

Birmingham Town Hall, c. 1900.
(Author's collection)

First published 2012

The History Press
The Mill, Brimscombe Port
Stroud, Gloucestershire, GL5 2QG
www.thehistorypress.co.uk

© Vanessa Morgan, 2012

The right of Vanessa Morgan to be identified as the Author
of this work has been asserted in accordance with the
Copyrights, Designs and Patents Act 1988.

British Library Cataloguing in Publication Data.
A catalogue record for this book is available from the British Library.

ISBN 978 0 7524 7153 2

Typesetting and origination by The History Press
Printed in Great Britain

CONTENTS

Acknowledgements

Research for this book was mainly undertaken using the local newspapers of the period. These included the *Birmingham Daily Post*, *Birmingham Mail*, *Birmingham Weekly Post*, and *Birmingham Aris Gazette*, all of which are held in the Birmingham Archives and Heritage Centre in Birmingham Library.

The Times Digital Archive also provided valuable help, showing the dates of these various crimes in order to pinpoint them in the local newspapers.

The census records and parish registers, also held in the Archives and Heritage Centre in Birmingham Library, assisted greatly in detailing specific addresses.

C.C.H. Moriarty's book *Birmingham City Police Centenary*, Monday, 20 November 1939, was of great help in compiling the history of Birmingham's criminal and judicial history.

Finally, without the help of the Midland Railway Society, I may never have discovered exactly where Edgbaston railway station was!

Birmingham Post Office, c. 1900. (Author's collection)

Introduction

It is hard to imagine the large, sprawling city of Birmingham as once being a small, manorial parish. But before the Industrial Revolution changed the face of Britain this was certainly the case.

The town was run by an ancient body known as the Court Leet. They consisted of a High Bailiff, a Low Bailiff and the Court Leet Jury, all local men of some standing. Every year they would appoint a Headborough and two constables. The Headborough, also known as the Prison Keeper, was in charge of the Public Office and was assisted by half-a-dozen men known as 'thief-takers'. The constables' job was to keep law and order.

As the town grew, the old manorial system became out-dated and the Improvement Acts and Street Acts of 1769 and 1773 gave limited control to a Board of Street Commissioners. It was their responsibility to keep the streets safe and they appointed street keepers and nightwatchmen to patrol the streets day and night. These men were provided with a uniform and equipment and were instructed to provide protection for people and property, and to also deal with traffic problems and obstructions.

Another body of law enforcers were the Justices of the Peace and the magistrates. They carried out their duties at the Public Office in Moor Street and in times of trouble would enrol special constables to assist the keepers and watchmen.

The old jailhouse was in Peck Lane, where New Street railway station now stands, but in 1806 a new gaol was built in Moor Street, next to the Public Office. This is now the site of Moor Street station.

By 1839 there were thirty street keepers and 180 nightwatchmen, but in the summer of this year the Chartist Riots took place. A hundred special constables were sworn in to try to supress the riots but they couldn't cope and re-enforcements from the Metropolitan Police in London were brought to help. Following this, an Act of Parliament was passed giving Birmingham permission to set up its own police force.

The last Headborough and constables were appointed on 25 October 1839. They were Mr George Redfern, who had been Headborough since 1811, William

No. of House	Name of Street, Place, or Road, and Name or No. of House	Name and Surname of each Person who abode in the house, on the Night of the 30th March, 1851	Relation to Head of Family	Condition	Age of Males	Age of Females	Rank, Profession, or Occupation	Where Born	Whether Blind, or Deaf-and-Dumb
8	9 Moor Street	Richard Tongue	Head	Mar	32		Porter	Shropshire Ludlow	✓
		Charlotte Do	Wife	Mar		33		do do	✓
		Mary Do	Daur			11	Scholar	do do	✓
		Richard Do	Son		X		At Home	do do	✓
		Henry do	Son		2			Warwickshire Birm	
		Sarah Ann do	Daur			months		do do	
9	Public Office Moor Street	George Glossop	Head	Mar	32		Police Officer	Oxfordsh Dorchester	
		Sarah do	Wife	Mar		36		Gloucestersh Bristol	
		Mary Ann do	Daur			7		Warwickshire Birm	
		Emily do				2		do Birm	
		Ann do	Mother	Mar				do Aston	
		Harriet Still	serv	U		19	Servant	Shropsh Shrewsbury	
		John Beaumont	Turnkey	Mar	39		Police Sergeant Turnkey	Gloucestersh Bristol	
		Elizabeth do	Wife	Mar		43	House Keeper	do Wotton under	
		James Turner	none	U	34		Police Constable	Warwicksh Fazeley	
		John Baker	"		33		do	Yorksh Rooton	
		Michael O'Hara	"		24		do	Ireland Count Down	
		Edwin Spink	"		28		do	Warwicksh Birm	
		Samuel Jarvis			29		do	Leicestersh Gibson	
		George Edw—			30			Radnorsh Old Radnor	

George Glossop listed on the 1851 census.
(HO107/2054/31/3. Held in Birmingham Archives and Heritage)

Corbett of New Street and Thomas Weston of High Street. Their appointment was short-lived as their positions were abolished on 20 November 1839.

A few months earlier, on 1 September 1839, Francis Burgess had been appointed as the first Police Commissioner for Birmingham. He was a barrister but had been in the 54th Foot Regiment from 1812 to 1817, and had been a captain at the Battle of Waterloo. He rented a house in Union Street for himself and his family and also established his office there, but moved to Waterloo Street in 1840.

It was Burgess' job to recruit a sufficient number of suitable men as police constables, and the local newspapers on 3 October 1839 printed an appeal for 'young men not over 36 or under 5' 8', able to read and write and produce testimonials of exceptional character.' By 30 November 1839, 260 men had been recruited following examinations by a police surgeon and an inspector from the Metropolitan Police. They were paid 17s a week and given a uniform. One shilling was deducted if lodgings had to be found for them. Members of the Metropolitan Police, who had remained in the town following the riots, left on 20 November and reported to the Home Office that the men 'cut a very good figure and seem to have made a good impression.'

On 25 November magistrates arranged to sit daily from that day onwards at 10 a.m. at the Public Office, Moor Street, to hear police cases.

Francis Burgess retired in September 1842. He thanked his new force for their excellent conduct and hoped that they would continue to maintain the same high character under the new governing body. This new governing body, known as the

Watch Committee, comprised of the mayor along with a selection of aldermen and councillors. Richard A. Stephens was appointed as the first Chief Superintendent. When he retired in 1860, the position was given to George Glossop. George had been one of the original members of the force, having joined as a constable in November 1839.

By 1849, Moor Street Gaol had become too small and so was replaced by Winson Green Prison, built by Daniel R. Hill. It has been altered and re-built many times over the years.

Before 1884, criminal cases from Birmingham were tried at Warwick Assizes, but in 1884 Birmingham became an assize town. The first cases were heard at the Council House on Monday 4 August before Baron Huddleston and Mr Justice Wills who were judges on the Midland Circuit. Baron Huddleston said, 'It was a matter of great congratulations that the calendar was very light. [That] there were no cases of brutal violence.' Those tried at the first assizes were John Reardon, a jeweller, for inciting William Fry to steal a quantity of jewellery from the Birmingham Mint, his employers, John Welch, for damaging shop windows and George Jones for offering counterfeit money.

The Council House, built between 1874 and 1879. (© V. Morgan)

The new Victoria Law Courts in Corporation Street were built to house the assizes in the late 1880s by Birmingham firm, John Bowen & Sons. The foundation stone was laid by Queen Victoria on 23 March 1887 and the courts were opened by the Prince and Princess of Wales on 12 July 1891. The building is now the Magistrates Court.

Sentence of death is what most criminals could expect before the nineteenth century and the sentence would always be carried out within forty-eight hours of the trial. But by the turn of the century it was usually only murderers who faced the hangman's noose and as the nineteenth century progressed their wait until that meeting lengthened to fourteen days.

The *Birmingham Daily Post* in April 1863 gave a summary of what life was like for a condemned man in the days following his trial:

From the moment of his condemnation until the period fixed for his execution a murderer is the most carefully tended inmate of a prison. The law is so jealous lest it should be cheated of its victim that he is watched night and day, without a momentary interval, by special warders. Perhaps it is a merciful consideration that the unhappy wretch is not left alone to brood over his own thoughts to count the weary moments; to listen to the deep clanging of the prison clock, and feel another hour of his life has flown.

But the law is still considerate. It gives to the murderer what he denied to his victim – time for preparation, for repentance. The chaplain of the gaol makes the murderer his special care, joining in most fervently in prayers daily offered to him.

Following the sitting of the Royal Commission on Capital Punishment from 1864-6, public hangings were abolished in 1868. Executions now took place behind the prison walls and a black flag was raised to let those waiting outside know the punishment had happened. People still gathered outside just to see that black flag. Initially, newspaper reporters were still allowed to watch the hanging and members of the victim's family were also invited. Although executions continued for many more years, the flying of the black flag ended in 1902.

Some fortunate criminals found that mitigating circumstances averted them from making that sad journey to the scaffold, as some of the following cases show. So let me now take you to meet some of these characters and judge for yourselves whether their sentences were just, or whether some did actually get away with murder …

Vanessa Morgan, 2012

'Destruction to the present government'

1791

Suspects:	*Francis Field and John Green*
Age:	*Unknown*
Charge:	*Rioting*
Sentence:	*Execution*

In the summer of 1791 Birmingham was described as a place 'where all the wealthy and principle inhabitants were dissenters'. They were said to be poisoning the minds of the lower classes with wild ideas of abolishing the Crown and establishing the 'Rights of Man'. One of these men was Joseph Priestley, a minister of the New Unitarian Meeting

Temple Row. (© V. Morgan)

House and a strong supporter of the French Revolution. He preached, it was said, 'with the spirit of animated republicanism'.

On 11 June 1791, an announcement appeared in the local newspaper inviting like-minded people to a dinner at the Dadley & Co. Hotel in Temple Row, to celebrate the second anniversary of the storming of the Bastille: 'Any Friend to Freedom disposed to join the intended temperate festivity is desired to leave his name at the bar of the Hotel, where tickets may be had at five shillings each.'

Handbills were distributed saying, 'My Countrymen: the second year of the Gallic Liberty is nearly expired; at the commencement of the third, on the 14th of this month, it is devoutly to be wished that every enemy to civil and religious despotism, would give his sanction to the majestic common cause, by public celebration of the anniversary.' It went on to remind the populace of the enthusiasm aroused when the Bastille, 'that high altar and castle of despotism', fell, and to describe Parliament as 'venal', ministers as 'hypocritical', the clergy as 'legal oppressors' and the Crown as 'too weighty for the head that wears it'.

Questions were raised as to whether the bill was a forgery or if it was a scheme to raise a mob for the purpose of plunder. Unfortunately, it proved to be the latter. As the eighty-one guests arrived at 3 p.m. on that Thursday afternoon, they were greeted by a small crowd of protestors. At first these protestors were peaceful, merely jeering and booing at the diners, but then through the windows they heard the first toast – 'destruction to the present government and the King's head upon a charger.' The crowd rushed into the hotel, breaking windows, furniture and glasses, and throwing stones at the guests as they made their escape. The damage amounted to £144 11s 11d.

From the hotel, a group made their way to Priestley's meeting house, where they tore down the pulpit, made a bonfire of the contents and then set fire to the building. Another group went to his house at Fair Hill, two miles away, and set fire to it. They also made an effigy of him which they hung up and burned. Ironically, despite fervently preaching against the luxuries of life and the use of strong liquor, which he said was vulgar, his cellar was found to be filled with wine. The rioters helped themselves and became intoxicated.

As word spread, more people joined the rioters. At seven o'clock that evening they held a meeting behind the Swan Inn to choose dwelling houses and meeting houses for destruction. Meanwhile, the magistrates Joseph Charles and Dr Spencer swore in as many constables as they could, and soldiers from the Oxford Blues were ordered to march to Birmingham.

The riots continued through Friday and Saturday but by Sunday morning the town was said to be quiet, apart from twenty men lying drunk on the green. However, as soon as the morning services ended, the riots began again. By Sunday evening the damage amounted to £250,000, and, with no business having been transacted since Thursday, an estimated loss of about £3,000 revenue.

John Ryland's house at Easy Hill was burnt down because his son had helped Priestley to escape. Mr Humphrey's house at the turnpike was pulled down. He had offered the mob 8,000 guineas to spare it, but the rioters said money wasn't their object. Dr Withring was the first surgeon in Birmingham, but he was a dissenter, so wasn't spared. His house was pulled down on Sunday evening.

Other principal houses demolished or set on fire were – the Old and New Meeting Houses in Birmingham, Revd Coult's and Mr Ryland's at Five Ways, Moseley Hall in Bordesely (the property of John Taylor the co-founder of the bank Taylor Lloyds, now Lloyds TSB), Mr Hobson's in Balsall Heath, Mr Russell's in Shovel Green, Mr Hanwood's in King's Heath and in nearby Moseley, Mr Hawkes Jnr's, Mr Budd's and Mr Harwood's.

The rioters were very organised in the ways they attacked the buildings: If a house was detached, it would be set on fire; if semi-detached, the doors and windows were broken and the furniture taken out into the street, piled up and set alight. While doing all this they continually chanted 'God Save the King', 'Long Live the King, Church and State,' or 'Down with Dissenters'.

Where the house belonged to a dissenter but the inhabitant was an Anglican, notice was given for him to remove his contents and, if needed, help was given before the house was destroyed. John Taylor was with his family in Cheltenham at the time of the riots, but Lady Carhampton, the mother of the Duchess of Cumberland, was residing at his Birmingham property. Assistance was given and her goods removed and she was taken in by Sir Robert Lawley. The rioters then helped themselves to Mr Taylor's liquor and in no time the mansion house was in flames.

In an effort to put an end to the destruction, a bill was distributed reminding the rioters that the cost of the repairs would be charged to the respective parishes and would be paid out of the rates. This would bring extra taxation which the rioters, and others in the years to come, would feel. But still the riots continued.

Reports said that Joseph Priestley had escaped to Kidderminster but it seemed that the rioters would not stop until all the dissenters had left Birmingham. It was the arrival of re-enforcements from Nottingham which finally dispersed the mob. Elliot's Light Horse regiment left Nottingham at eight o'clock on Sunday morning and arrived in Birmingham at ten o'clock that night. They were said to be covered in dust and much fatigued. A magistrate read the Riot Act, while the troops rested at the Swan Inn for the night.

By the morning the rioters had left for Worcestershire, and, although the soldiers followed, they had scattered.

Over the coming weeks there was a lot of debate as to who was to blame for the riots, how they took hold so quickly and why they took so long to quell. The dissenters felt the government hadn't done enough. As a token gesture, a few arrests of known rioters were made and these men appeared at the Warwick Assizes on Tuesday, 23 August 1791.

Francis Field of Aston was charged with burning John Taylor's house and was found guilty. Three witnesses, Edward Cotterill, Samuel Healey and John Brookes, said they had seen Field start the fire. He was seen at nine o'clock at night walking up the gravel path and entering the house. He went upstairs, where the floor was wooden, carrying flaming torches from the hall and then carried more to another room and then again to the first-floor landing. He fed the fires with paper hangings and furniture. John Green was charged with helping him and both were found guilty.

William Rice of Aston was charged with having 'assembled unlawfully to riot and disturb the public peace, and to demolish the dwelling house of William Hutton in Washwood Heath'. Two witnesses, George Rowell and George Mascall, said they had seen him there, but he called two other witnesses who could prove he was elsewhere and so he was acquitted.

Robert Whitehead of Aston was charged in regards to William Hutton's house. Witnesses said they saw him knocking the windows out with bludgeons and committing other acts of violence. But another witness said that Robert was actually a friend of Hutton's and when Hutton's picture of Garrick as King Lear was thrown from the window Robert rescued it – he was found not guilty.

The court was seen as being so lenient on the rioters that the phrase 'nothing but a Birmingham jury can save you' came into common parlance. Of course, this isn't strictly true as the assizes took place in Warwick.

In the end, only three rioters were sentenced to death – Francis Field, Bartholomew Fisher and John Green. They were said to have acted penitently and acknowledged their crimes, though claimed that they would not have become involved had it not been for the seditious handbill that had been published. On the day before his execution Bartholomew Fisher received a pardon. The other two were not so lucky and kept their appointment with the hangman.

The Walls were Stained with Blood

1828

Suspect:	Edward Roach
Age:	Unknown
Charge:	Murder
Sentence:	Committed suicide to escape justice

The first half of the nineteenth century saw a large influx of people into Birmingham from the surrounding area, looking for work in this now growing industrial town. These people needed homes and so many back-to-back courts were constructed. These houses were inexpensive to build and quickly spread across the town. They were also cheap to live in, but accommodation was basic in the extreme. There were only two or three rooms in each house, with thin walls separating the individual families and shared toilet and washing facilities. Over-crowding was a common problem, but the difficult and cramped conditions often meant that friendly, close-knit communities developed.

Edward Roach, a whip maker, and his wife, Mary, lived in one of these courts at the back of 17 Ellis Street, Birmingham with their three children. Edward and Mary had been married about eight years and had lived in Ellis Street for about four months. Everyone who knew him said Edward had seemed a man of good character and that they had only seen him intoxicated three times.

But recently Edward had renewed an intimacy with a female residing in Exeter Row. He had been attracted

The only remaining back-to-backs in Birmingham today. They have been renovated and are cared for by the National Trust. (© V. Morgan)

Ellis Street today. (© V. Morgan)

to her before his marriage but, at the time, she had only been sixteen years old. Naturally, Mary was jealous and had taken to quarrelling with him over it.

On 15 October 1828 Elizabeth Pearson, whose house in Court No.3 adjoined the Roach's building, heard cries of 'Murder!' and the children screaming. The next morning she asked Mary what had happened and Mary showed her marks on her neck, which looked as if someone had tried to strangle her. She also had a black eye.

On Saturday, 29 November 1828, Edward was at work as usual and approached a fellow workman, William Mansell, and asked him to sharpen his knife. He said he wanted it done straight away because he needed it to work with. William obliged and although previously Edward had always left his knife in the shop, on this particular day he took it home with him.

The next evening, neighbours heard loud quarrelling between Edward and Mary. Henry Hawkins, a malster who lived at No. 17 and described the walls between the two homes as being quite thin, heard Mary call out, 'Oh my dear husband, don't!' several times. He also heard her scream 'Murder!' and then a noise as if both had fallen down the stairs.

He rushed round and could hear Mary trying to get out of the house. He knocked and called for them to open the door, but no one replied. Then he heard Edward going up the stairs. Other neighbours now arrived and Mary could be heard groaning on the other side of the door, but no one could open it and so they sent for the nightwatchman.

John Price, the watchman, was on his rounds and was checking that the new canal office had been locked up properly, when a boy rushed up saying that a murder had been committed at the back of Ellis Street. When he arrived at the house he found what he described as 'a great number of people round the door, which was closely fastened'. After failing to open the door, he removed the grating to get in through the cellar door. By now another nightwatchman who had been patrolling Exeter Street had arrived and followed Price inside.

There was no light in the house but by the light of his lantern John Price found Mary Roach. He was so horror-struck that he screamed out. She was laying on her back behind the front door and was surrounded by a dark pool of blood. Her face had been slashed in many places, her neck perforated and her arm was only hanging on by a piece of skin. On the kitchen table lay a knife dripping with blood. It was eighteen inches long, with a thirteen-inch blade and two-and-a-half-inches wide. This was the knife Edward had asked William Mansell to sharpen for him.

By now William Baldwin, the night constable, had arrived and John Price opened a window for him to get in. Then they heard a gunshot upstairs. Going up, they found the bedroom still filled with smoke from the gunshot. Edward Roach was lying on the bed, his head partly slumped over the headboard and blood oozing from a wound in his right temple. Some described him as having his brains scattered thickly over his shoulders. His three children were on the bed with him. The youngest, who was said to be about two years old, was lying by his arm. The other two, who were aged six and four, were sitting up and smiling but when everyone started coming into the room they began to cry.

The inquest was held in the Wellington Tavern, Exeter Row, before the coroner, Mr Whateley. Before the proceedings began the jury were taken to view the house and the bodies. Reporters went with them and the local newspaper gave graphic descriptions of the scene:

On entering the house the first thing we perceived was a pool of blood inside the front door, the walls were also stained with blood and the floor crimsoned with the same. The body of Mary Roach lay on a board on the floor; it had no covering but a slight chemise, which was literally dyed in her blood. Her face was also very much stained with gore. Her right arm lay partially extended and presented a horrible appearance it being almost cut in two at the elbow. Several wounds appeared on her head. On a table near the body a knife was found with which the deed was perpetrated. The deceased was below the middle size; aged about 27. On proceeding up stairs to the bedroom, we observed the stairs quite wet and even slippery with blood, the walls were also quite saturated. A pool of blood was at the threshold of the bedroom.

On the bedstead, which had little or no bed-clothes on it, the body of Edward Roach lay extended. He had his waistcoat, shirt, pantaloons and stockings on him. His head was hung over the headboard of the bed. Underneath it there was a quantity of blood, which had run in different directions along the boards. The jury having viewed the bodies, returned to the inquest.

A surgeon, Mr Covey, examined the bodies. He described his findings on Mary's body, saying that all the muscles and tendons in her forearm had been completely severed and two bones were also dislocated. There were four wounds on her head: one at the back which had penetrated the skull, a deep one over the right ear which was an inch long, and two small scalp wounds. There was also a large cut on her back between the shoulder blade and the spine. She was two months' pregnant. Death was through extensive loss of blood.

He stated that the right side of Edward's face was completely shattered by the gunshot and that death would have been instantaneous.

Edward was buried late at night on the following Wednesday in St Bartholomew's burial ground, as was the custom with suicides. Mary's body was returned to her relatives and was buried at St Mary's, Whittal Street, on 6 December.

What happened to the children following this tragedy is uncertain but, according to reports, they were 'left unprotected by their father's dreadful crime'. The youngest child, Matilda, seems to have been taken in at an address in Bromsgrove Street and was baptised at St Philip's on 1 January 1829. Her parents are given as Edward and Mary Roach, a whip maker, but no mention is made of them being deceased. She and Maria appear on the 1841 census as servants – Maria at Brook Street and Matilda at Harborne Road, Edgbaston. Matilda married Thomas Maden at All Saints' on 7 February 1853 and at some point went to live in London, as in 1871 she is a widow in Marylebone. It is known that her father was born in London of Irish parents, so perhaps she found some relatives there. The eldest son, Edward, completely disappears.

SOLVED

'That devil Davenport is my greatest enemy'

1838

Suspect:	William Devey
Age:	Twenty-eight
Charge:	Murder
Sentence:	Execution

Little Hampton Street. (© V. Morgan)

'On Wednesday evening the neighbourhood of Snow Hill and Little Hampton Street was thrown into a state of great excitement by the perpetration of a most determined murder.' So reported the *Birmingham Journal* in April 1838.

Twenty-eight-year-old William Devey was a spoon-maker and lived almost opposite Joseph Davenport, the licensed victualler at the Pheasant Inn. They had, according to all accounts, been on friendly terms until Davenport appeared as a witness in a case brought against William Devey by a Mr Rowley, for 'seducing a hired servant from his employment'. Davenport appeared as a witness for Rowley and when Devey lost and was ordered to pay damages of 40s, he blamed Davenport for it. A 'distress' was then levied on Devey's premises by the Gas Light Company and William was again convinced it was Joseph Davenport's fault.

On Wednesday, 4 April 1838, at about three o'clock, Devey went into a gunsmith's in Weaman Street owned by Miss Emma David and her sister, Caroline Webley, and purchased a brace of pistols and twenty-eight bullets. He said he wanted them for a friend and was most particular in asking how to load them correctly and use them properly, as he needed to show his friend.

Later, he met Benjamin Clulee on Snows Hill. 'I'm glad to meet thee – come and have a glass with me,' he said. Clulee claimed he had already had one but was persuaded by Devey to have another and so they went into the Salutation Inn.

Devey bought Clulee a gin and water but didn't have one himself. He pulled out three sovereigns and some silver saying, 'You see, I am not ruined yet'. He then began relating his anger over Davenport, 'That devil Davenport is my greatest enemy, although I have been his best friend. What do you think he did? Why, he sent round to all my creditors to give them notice to come in or they would have nothing for I was going to sell off.' Clulee said that he didn't believe Davenport would do such a thing. But Devey was determined to have his revenge. 'Revenge be damned,' said Clulee, 'attend to your business.'

Devey left the pub about 6.30 p.m. and a short time later he found Davenport in Batkin's, an ironmonger's, where the assistant, Samuel Farrington, heard Davenport ask, 'Why do you follow me? What have I done to you?'

Devey replied, 'Damn your eyes, you have been the ruin of me and now I will settle this.' He raised a pistol and fired. When it misfired, Davenport tried to escape into the parlour at the back of the shop but Devey followed him and fired again with another pistol. This time he didn't miss and Davenport fell to the floor, dead. Mr Leeson, who lived next door, heard the commotion and seized Devey as he was leaving, saying 'Come Devey, this game will never do.'

'Very well,' Devey replied. 'You may do what you like with me.' He threw one pistol in the gutter and dropped the other at his feet. As Leeson stooped to pick the latter up, Devey grabbed a shoemaker's knife which was on the counter and cut his own throat. James Welsh, who was passing the shop, caught him as he fell and heard him say, 'I resign myself. I shall die happy.'

Devey was taken to hospital where his wound, which had cut through the windpipe, was said to be serious but treatable. He was told the wound would heal if he was quiet but he pleaded with the doctor to let him die, 'If not, I shall be hanged for I have murdered a man. I have shot him.'

He warned his friends who visited him in hospital to keep away from public houses and gave instructions for his family. He said his effects were to be sold off for the benefit of his wife and child, and that certain premises might be appropriated to his creditors. On recovery, he was transported to Warwick Gaol to await his trial at the Summer Assizes.

This took place on 9 August 1838 and the newspapers reported that, 'The trial of this case excited great interest in this part of the country and caused the court to be crowded to excess.' At the start of the proceedings Devey showed an appearance of a decent tradesman but as the trial progressed, he appeared to become more and more aware of his situation.

Mr Brindley, the doctor at the hospital who had examined Davenport's body, said there was a circular wound the size of a coin with a lot of coagulated blood. The shot had passed through the skull near the middle of the head and then through the brain.

The defence, a Mr Hill, tried to prove insanity and produced several witnesses who said that Devey had been acting strangely during the previous months and that he had been suffering from delusions as to the conduct of Davenport. He also told how several members of Devey's family had suffered from unsound minds; two aunts and a cousin had died insane and his sister had tried to commit suicide twice. Devey himself had also attempted self-destruction. Two servants said his manner had changed since the Rowley case – he had sent for a man to mend a tub when no tubs needed mending and another to cast metal, when no metal needed casting. His two brothers claimed he had not been in his right mind since April. A doctor said that he had treated him for delusion and that Devey had also asked him to open up his chest to investigate a bad cough that he had had.

However, even if they acquitted him on grounds of insanity, Mr Hill agreed that he should not be set free as he posed a danger to others.

The counsel for the prosecution, Mr Gailburn, brought neighbours as witnesses who said they hadn't noticed anything unusual with him, and he reminded the jury that 'they must not forget their obligation for the protection of the public'.

The jury took just a few minutes to find William Devey guilty of murder, whereupon the judge gave the death sentence and ordered that Devey's body be buried within the precincts of the gaol. At this, the prisoner begged that as he had no recollection of having committed the crime, he hoped his Lordship would allow him to be buried amongst his relations. The judge refused.

Friends immediately set about putting together a petition asking for a remission on grounds of insanity, but after perusing the petition Lord John Russell said that he could not see sufficient grounds for a reprieve and the execution warrant was signed.

The day before his execution William Devey was visited by his wife and other members of his family. It was said that his wife had only just given birth and was in a weak state, and she was so distressed that she had to be carried from the cell after saying her final goodbyes.

On the morning of the execution Devey spent a long time in prayer. He asked for forgiveness and prayed that he would meet Davenport in heaven. As he was led to the scaffold he said he hoped that his relations would help with the upkeep of his children and teach them to be law-abiding and virtuous. He ascended the platform and the rope was placed around his neck. Again he prayed that he should meet his victim in another and better world and as he cried out, 'Assist me! Oh assist me, Heavenly Father!' the platform fell and he died with hardly a struggle.

Five thousand people attended Devey's execution on 24 August.

SOLVED

Case Four

'Where you go, I will go'

1838

Suspect:	Abraham Holyoake
Age:	Twenty
Charge:	Murder
Sentence:	Acquitted

Six months after William Devery was executed, the *Birmingham Journal* reported another murder: 'The neighbourhood of Milk Street has this week been thrown into a state of considerable excitement in consequence of the death of a young woman named Evans, under extraordinary circumstances.' But was it murder?

Meriden Street today. (© V. Morgan)

Ann Maria Evans and Abraham Holyoake had lived in adjacent streets in Digbeth for quite a number of years. Ann was twenty-three years old and lived with her mother, Frances, and stepfather, William Jones, in Milk Street, Birmingham and worked at James James' screw manufacturers in Bradford Street. Abraham Holyoake, aged twenty, lived with his father in Meriden Street and worked for his father as a file cutter. He was described as being of good character.

Milk Street today. (© V. Morgan)

Ann and Abraham had been 'keeping company' for over two years, but friends said he had been more constant in his attention to Ann over the last couple of months.

On the Monday evening of 29 October 1838 Abraham and Ann went to a dance together at the Malt Shovel in Milk Street. It seems that Holyoake had bestowed more notice upon some girl in the room than was pleasant to his intended, and an argument erupted between the couple. Ann said she didn't want anything more to do with Abraham and the following morning she refused to see him. But it seems that by the afternoon she had forgiven him as he spent the evening at her house in the company of the lodgers Henry and Elizabeth Hodgkins. After they went to bed, Abraham and Ann were left alone.

At one o'clock in the morning, Mrs Jones came down to make a cup of tea and was surprised to see Abraham still there. 'It is quite time, Abraham, that you were gone home and my daughter was in bed,' she said. Through the thin walls the lodgers then heard her say, 'Ann, shake him [to see] if he's asleep or pretending,' and, 'Abraham you are going or if you don't I will charge the watchman with you.'

Abraham agreed to leave and Ann went to see him off. When her mother had made her cup of tea she looked out of the door and saw them in the entry. Again she told Abraham to go home and Ann to come to bed. Then she went back to bed herself.

An hour later James Jones, the night constable for Deritend, was walking along Great Barr Street when he heard a cry for help coming from the Warwick Canal. On reaching its banks he found Abraham standing on the tow path looking quite exhausted and soaking wet. Jones took Abraham by the arm and asked what the matter was. When he only received a groan for reply, he asked Abraham why he had been in the canal. 'Are you drunk or have you fallen in by accident?' They were then joined by the nightwatchman, Robert Wood, and Abraham told them he had lost his hat and his handkerchief in the water. Then he said, 'Oh dear, the woman'.

Horrified that there was a woman in the water, they asked if he had had a lady with him. 'Yes', he said, and explained that they had been in the water together, but she

The canal and railway bridge at Great Barr Street. (© V. Morgan)

had got out and gone home. Both Jones and Wood thought this seemed strange. They couldn't understand why she would just go home and leave him on his own in the canal, so they asked him if he had drowned her. Abraham said he hadn't, but he was agitated, which made them suspicious, so they insisted he take them to her house to make sure she was all right.

On their way to Milk Street he became more agitated as more questions were asked – Why had they both been out so late? Why were they in the water? In the end, Abraham admitted he had drowned Ann in the canal and told them they would find her body on the Birmingham side of the bridge in Great Barr Street.

However, after Ann's body had been found, Abraham changed his story, saying, 'Oh dear, she is dead and we intended to die together.' Asked what he meant, he said that she had had an argument with her mother so they had mutually agreed to drown themselves. She had jumped in and he had followed.

The inquest was held at the Sailor's Return public house. Before its conclusion, the newspapers were already implying that this was a murder case, mainly due to the fact that Abraham had not died – 'himself being saved from death which he says was mutually agreed upon, is at least sufficient to excite suspicions and to call for the most searching questions.' There was also the question of why Abraham had changed his story.

Meanwhile, Abraham wasn't saying anything – except that he had done wrong and must answer for it. He would sooner die than live. At the inquest he sat with his head bowed, almost touching his knees.

The jury went to view the body, which was being kept in the loft of the inn. They commented on the fact there were no visible injuries, then returned to hear the evidence.

Both Jones and Wood, and then Hodgkins gave their evidence, and a boatman said he had heard a lot of quarrelling on the banks of the canal at the time of the drowning. Ann's mother said she had never heard Ann talk of doing harm to herself. She did admit that Ann was a 'random-speaking girl', but maintained she never really thought of actually carrying out what she threatened.

Finally, Abraham told how he had tried to persuade Ann to go home but she had kept repeating, 'Where you go, I will go'. When he had left the house in Milk Street he had wanted to go for a walk, but Ann said that he should stay with her a little longer. They had walked along the tow path to the Great Barr Street bridge, where Abraham once again told Ann to go home. But again she had said, 'Where you go, I will go'. Abraham had then said, 'Well, here goes then' and had jumped into the canal. Ann had duly followed him.

Mr Wateley, the coroner, said that the law stated that if two persons agreed to commit suicide, but one survived, then that survivor was guilty of murder. The jury found Abraham guilty of wilful murder and he was taken to Warwick Gaol to await the next assizes.

Abraham's trial took place on Tuesday, 2 April 1839, before Mr Justice Bosenquet, and from the start it appeared that no one in court thought there was a case to be tried. The judge said he had read over the evidence and felt the facts did not warrant a verdict against the prisoner. Even the council for prosecution, Mr Balguy, seemed to think Abraham had only changed his story because he was bewildered and confused. Although he had been drinking with the Hodgkins' at Ann's house, there was no evidence that he was drunk. And there was no motive; they had not quarrelled and there was no feeling of jealousy between them (it seems the argument over Abraham's flirting at the dance had been forgotten).

Mr Hill, for the defence, thanked both for their humane view and said that Abraham would 'never cease to deplore having been the cause, however unintentionally, of the death of a being to whom he had looked forward as the future companion of his life, and as one destined to bless the remainder of his days with happiness'.

Mr Justice Bosenquet advised the jury to bring a verdict of not guilty – which they did.

'Never cease to deplore', Mr Hill had said. Now, Abraham is quite an unusual name and Holyoake is not an exceptionally common surname, so his whereabouts can be traced using records. He lived in Meriden Road and, in 1851, at No. 64 Meriden Road there is an Abraham Holyoake with a wife Isabella and four children. They had married in 1840 and went on to have nine children between 1843 and 1857.

Abraham died in early 1888, aged sixty-nine, and one wonders how often during his lifetime did he feel the remorse his defence lawyer suggested he would.

Case Five

'Where are the police?'

1839

Suspects: Chartist supporters

Ages: Various

Charges: Rioting and criminal damage

Sentences: Various

The bronze statue of Thomas Attwood, which has sat on the steps of Chamberlain Square since 1993. (© V. Morgan)

The Chartists were a movement of working men who strove for social and economic reform. William Lovett, the secretary of the movement, wrote the People's Charter, requesting a change in parliamentary elections to give all men the right to vote. Thomas Attwood, Birmingham's first MP, sympathised with the movement and campaigned for parliamentary reform. On 14 June 1839 he presented a petition to Parliament but it was rejected and he resigned.

The Chartists began meeting in large towns in their multitudes, listening to speeches from people from all over the country. After meetings in Newcastle, Manchester and Leeds they headed for Birmingham, where they began to assemble on 1 July 1839. To quell any possible riots, Lord John Russell despatched sixty men from the Metropolitan Police Force and they

The remains of St Thomas' Church: a victim of the bombs of the Second World War. (© V. Morgan)

arrived by train at 8 p.m. on the Tuesday evening. They then travelled by omnibus to the Bull Ring, where the Chartists had already begun to assemble, holding flags and banners - one showing the death's head and crossbow.

Holloway Head. In the distance, the spire of St Martin's can be seen in the Bull Ring, where the Chartists marched to. (© V. Morgan)

Birmingham's mayor, Mr W. Scholefield, rode on horseback to the front of what was now being called a 'mob'. He asked them to disperse; they ignored him and so he signalled to the police standing at the end of Moor Street to advance. They moved into the crowd, seizing the flags and banners. This angered the Chartists, who began attacking the police and breaking flag poles in order to make weapons. One policeman got separated from his colleagues and was immediately surrounded by about forty protestors. He was a powerful man and initially managed to keep them at bay but then he slipped and fell, dropping his staff. The Chartists rushed at him and bludgeoned him. Other policemen tried to rescue him but were beaten off. The constable managed to get up and stagger to St Martin's wall, but there he was stabbed and fell, to a great cheer from the crowd.

The 4th Dragoons now arrived and forced the crowd down Digbeth, up Bromsgrove Street and then to St Thomas' Church. Cornered, the mob tore the iron palisades from the walls of the church and used them as weapons to attack both the Dragoons and the police.

One man left behind in the Bull Ring threw a stone at a soldier who rode past him. The soldier grabbed him by the collar, threw him across his horse and took him to the gaol – to the applause of the town's inhabitants, who were watching from their windows.

By 11.30 p.m. all had gone quiet.

The former Public Office on Moor Street, now a slip road around the railway station.

The magistrates convened early in the morning and many who had been arrested the night before were brought before them. These included John Taylor, often referred to as Dr Taylor, a staunch supporter of the movement. He was charged with addressing 'a number of people some time after the Riot Act had been read.' Others included William Shears, John Neale, Edward Hughes, John Story, John Rhodes, Thomas King and Frederick Mason. By 7.30 a.m. they had been sent to Warwick Gaol.

The situation seemed to quieten down and for a couple of weeks everything went back to normal – until Monday 15 July.

A rumour was circulated that Thomas Attwood was coming to Birmingham to hold a meeting at Holloway Head, and so small groups of Chartists began to make their way there. By 2 p.m. about 2,000 had congregated.

They appeared quite peaceful as they lay stretched out on the grass, some smoking their dingy tobacco pipes while a number of boys played pitch and toss. But small groups gradually began to move away, once again, to the Bull Ring and shops were forced to close not only in the Bull Ring but also in neighbouring Edgbaston Street and Exeter Row as stones were thrown through windows.

Whether Thomas Attwood intended coming is not known, but he failed to make an appearance and after speeches made by other members of the Chartists, the remaining spectators were asked to form a line, six abreast, and move down to Suffolk Street, in order to show the authorities that they could act in a peaceable and orderly fashion.

However, instead of following the instructions, they rushed to the Bull Ring, which they now considered to be their rallying point, chanting, 'The police dare not face us!' and 'The soldiers dare not face us!' Amongst the chanting could be heard the sounds of breaking glass as windows were shattered and the palisades were broken in Bradford Street and High Street in Deritend. The mob, now armed with iron and wooden bludgeons, then proceeded along Moor Street to the Public Office. In minutes, every window in the front of this building was demolished.

What made it worse was the fact that the London police had been given orders by the magistrates not to act without their command, so they were powerless to stop them. So now, unrestrained, the mob returned to the Bull Ring. Here they dug up the pavement stones and threw them around with considerable force. They pulled out the iron railings which surrounded Nelson's monument and used them to batter down doors and shutters. In five minutes hardly a windowpane was left intact.

The windows and shutters of Bournes, the wholesale grocer's, were broken and the mob entered the shop. Tea chests and tin canisters were thrown out into the street and demolished. Mr Leggett, the feather-merchant, had his chairs, tables, feather-beds and linen made into a bonfire in the centre of the Bull Ring. Fragments of the burning materials were then thrown into the shops and soon the buildings were engulfed in flames. An elegant lamp above the shop door of Mr Wainwright the liquor merchant, only recently put up, was demolished. Burning fragments from the bonfire were thrust through the shop doors of Mrs Brinton and Mr Arnold. Jeweller, Mr Horton, had valuable goods kicked around the street or used as weapons – silver candlesticks were used to smash the windows of Mr Parkes' tobacconists shop. Mr Belcher and his servant had to be rescued through the upstairs window with ladders, after a fire was started in his shop. The terrified inhabitants demanded 'Where are the police?', 'Where are the military?' and 'Where are the magistrates?' In total sixteen shops, plus the Nelson Hotel, were destroyed. Three had miraculously escaped harm. These belonged to Mr Weston, Mr Ford and Mr Aston; three men who were described in reports as 'radicals'.

At 9.45 p.m. the police and military finally arrived and the mob fled in all directions. But the fires raged for most of the night.

The next morning reports told that, 'The streets presented an awful spectacle, crowded with men, women and children, intermingled with military and police.' No shops were open and some factories were also closed. Magistrates offered a £100 reward for the arrest of those involved in the burning of Bournes and Leggat's houses. The government offered a £200 reward and free pardons to anyone who could give information as to who was involved in the riots.

Despite all the destruction, only one man died in the riots. John Binnion was stabbed in the neck by a dragoon while trying to escape and died later on 1 August. His blood could be traced from Union Street to Dr Booth's surgery in Temple Row. The coroner returned a verdict of 'legally justifiable homicide'.

A petition was sent to Lord John Russell signed by fifty of the principle residents, complaining that they had been left unprotected and that the mayor and the magistrates were guilty of gross dereliction of duty. Lord Russell sent a reply requesting proof that 'previous information was given to the magistrates of the intention of the rioters'. In their defence, the mayor wrote back, saying that the magistrates had only left the Public Office after looking at the evidence and finding that it appeared to be just rumours, as before, but that they had left instructions that at the slightest sign of any disturbance they were to be sent for immediately. He added that the rioting started so suddenly that by the time the magistrates had returned, it was too late.

Thirty people were arrested and brought before the magistrates, including a man called Wilkes. The newspapers stated that he 'has been twice convicted of obstructing the passage of High Street by reading newspapers from Nelson's monument [and] has again been taken into custody for being present in the Bull Ring during the fires.'

The trials took place on 27 July 1839 and the men found guilty were sentenced on 15 August. Jeremiah Howell (thirty-one), Francis Roberts (twenty-six), John Jones (twenty-one) and Thomas Aston (fifteen) were sentenced to death for 'Feloniously demolishing a house [as a] Chartist'. These sentences were later commuted to transportation and they left for Australia in 1840. William Lovett and John Collins, the leader of the Birmingham branch of Chartists, both received twelve months for 'Seditious libel [as a] Chartist'. Other sentences for rioting varied from one month to eighteen months.

Case Six

Tied up in a Sack

1839

Suspect: Thomas Walsh

Age: Seventy

Charge: Murder

Sentence: Transportation

John Bill was a labourer who lived at 119 New St John Street. On Saturday, 14 December 1839, at seven o'clock in the morning, he was repairing and cleaning the highway around Witton Viaduct in Aston when he noticed a sack lying in the ditch. At first he thought it was a sack of potatoes but on closer investigation he spotted a hand lying across the top of the sack. He touched the hand with his rake and said, 'Hello friend, what makes you lie there?' There was no answer and when he touched the hand he found it was stiff and cold and realised it was a dead body. The lower part of the body was tied up inside the sack while another bag was pinned around the head.

He went to tell Mr Roberts, the parish clerk, who sent for Robert Dodds, the Headborough of Aston. They then returned to the body and pulled it out of the ditch. On removing the bag from around the head they found it was the body of an old man. He had a wound on his forehead and his hair was saturated with blood. The left arm of his jacket was also soaked with blood, as if he had been lying in a pool of blood before being put in the sack.

There was nothing in his pockets except a few buttons and a piece of string. Inspectors Hall and Stephens went about making enquiries and the body was taken to the bone house in Aston churchyard. (Due to the lack of space in the churchyards, old graves would be dug up to make room for new bodies and a 'bone house' was the building used to store the extracted bones.)

Eventually, Catherine Pemberton, the wife of Joseph Pemberton of Lawley Street, came forward, thinking she knew who it was and was taken to view the body. She recognised it as 'the old ragman'. She didn't know his name, but knew that he lived in one of the courts down the street opposite her. Further investigation established the body to be that of Peter Coffrey – Peter the ragman – a hard-working man who collected rags and bone. He was an Irishman and lived with his brother-in-law, Thomas Walsh, in Johnson's Court, Hop Pole Yard off Lawley Street.

An overgrown spot in the churchyard which hides the foundations of the old bone house. (© V. Morgan)

Thomas Walsh said he hadn't seen his brother-in-law since Thursday afternoon at around four o'clock, when he had said he was going to Coleshill to collect rag and bone and would stay in a lodging house for the night. But neighbours claimed that they thought they had seen Peter in the yard on the Friday afternoon. Catherine Pemberton said she was sure it was on the Friday because she had been washing on the Thursday and didn't go out of the front door at all that day. Ann Beach thought she had seen him on the Friday morning, around eight or nine o'clock, coming from the direction of the Priory, and Sarah Heath said she had seen him about an hour later, going up the yard with his bag thrown over his back.

When the police made a search of the house, Inspector Hall found a piece of brain matter with hair attached to it on the wall. He also found spots of blood on the wall around the fireplace and a large bloodstain under the floorboards. Burnt clothes, spotted with blood, were discovered in the fireplace and he also found a bloodstained hammer and a bloodstained stick. Thomas Walsh and his daughter, Ellen Connor, were taken in for questioning. Police also went to a house in Dale End where Walsh's son, John, and his wife, Mary, were also arrested. Walsh's other son, Owen, could not be found.

The inquest was held at the Aston Tavern before Mr J.W. Whateley on 16 December 1839. The jury and the reporters were taken to see the body, which was still being kept in the bone house.

The local newspaper reported that:

The body was drawn out of the bone house in the corner of the churchyard on a bier and presented a most horrifying spectacle. It is that of an old man apparently about 60 years of age dressed like a labourer with a large perforation in the centre of the forehead, surrounded with clotted blood and on turning him upon his face a smaller cavity was discovered in the back part of the skull through which the brain hung.

The four prisoners were described as 'sullen'. Thomas Walsh (seventy) maintained he was innocent. John (forty) said he would leave it to Almighty God. Ellen also asserted her innocence and Mary (forty) claimed she had never set foot in the house at all during the few weeks the family had been living there. The coroner ordered that they be taken to the prison in Moor Street while further investigations were made.

Neighbours said that Ellen had been seen thoroughly cleaning the house on the Saturday morning. She had her apron full of rushes, which she had thrown into the mixen-hole, and had washed the floors with a cloth. Sarah Bashford, the rent collector, said Walsh had paid the rent on Friday evening, even though it wasn't due until Monday. And Hannah Mills, licensee of the Seven Stars, said Thomas Walsh had gone into the Severn Stars and bought a half quart of rum.

The inquest was adjourned until 21 December but by this time three of the prisoners had made their confessions.

Firstly, Thomas Walsh admitted to having caused Peter's death. He said there had been an argument concerning the rent between himself and Peter on the Thursday night. Thomas said, 'He was not willing to pay the rent. I told him he should not remain in the house. He threw me down on the floor and lifted his knee on my chest. I told him not to kill me. He loosened me and as soon as I got up I took a bar of iron, like forge-tongs, and gave him a blow to the back of the head and killed him. My daughter was present but no one else. I threw the tongs into the canal and put him into a wagon which my son had brought to the house.'

John Walsh said that Owen had gone to his house saying, 'Oh my God, my father has killed Peter'. The next day, John went to his father's house and was shown Peter's body in the coal cellar. When John returned home from work later that afternoon, he found his cart was missing. His wife told him that his brother had taken it, and Owen brought it back later that night.

Ellen Connor cried continuously, saying, 'Nobody had a hand in it but my father.' She told how she had pleaded two or three times with them to stop arguing. She went upstairs to make the beds and had heard her father shout, 'Don't kill me!' When she came down she saw Peter stretched out on the floor.

By the time the family appeared at Warwick Assizes on 31 March 1840, Owen Walsh had still not been found.

The judge, Mr Justice Bosanquet, heard how Thomas and John had been seen bargaining for a hand wagon on the Thursday night and that a wagon had been seen being wheeled into the court by two men and a woman on the Friday night. Then wheeled away again, carrying something bulky.

Peter was known to have drawn some money from his account, and on the Saturday morning Mary Walsh had gone to the pawnbroker Alan Walton, in Dale End, and redeemed about a pound's worth of items belonging to her and John. Asked how she had come by the money she said her husband had sold some umbrellas.

Despite the evidence against all the prisoners, it was only Thomas who was found guilty. He was not given the death sentence but was ordered to be transported for life.

A convict ship, the *Eden*, sailed for New South Wales on 8 July 1840. After four months it arrived at its destination on 18 November 1840. The Convict Death Register records the burial of Thomas Walsh in Sydney on 20 November 1840.

'If I am to hang I shall die innocent'

1840

Suspect:	*Josiah Lilly*
Age:	*Seventeen*
Charge:	*Murder*
Sentence:	*Acquitted*

About eighteen months after the mysterious death of Ann Maria Evans, another girl was found in another part of the canal. Her death also aroused suspicion and one wonders if her sweetheart had remembered the story of Abraham Holyoake and concocted a similar story.

On Thursday, 7 May 1840, at four o'clock in the morning, boatman Thomas Morris was walking along the banks of the canal in Birmingham when he saw a man's hat lying on the towpath under the Walmer's Lane bridge. On further inspection he saw a woman's bonnet floating in the water. Thinking that there may be a body in the canal, he went back to his boat and fetched a hook, and, together with his brother, searched the waters. In no time they had pulled a girl's body out. They sent word to the police and, while waiting for the constable to arrive, they continued looking for a man's body, but didn't find one.

When Sergeant Brough arrived he searched the girl's clothing to try to discover her identity. In one of her pockets they found a letter sent

The bridge previously known as Walmer's Lane, now Lancaster Street. (© V. Morgan)

to her by a Josiah Lilley. It had been written on 22 April and sent from the House of Correction. It read:

> Dear Harriet. I hope you will receive these few lines with as much affection as they are sent. My condition must certainly be grievous to you; however, if you should have the affection for me which I believe you have, I should not have written to you, the time being so short, only that you should not think I had forgotten you. I hope I shall have the pleasure of receiving a letter from you, short as time is. You will please to let my mother know that you have heard from me, and ask her to send me some money to come out with, as I daresay you have none to spare, and even if you have I had rather it came from my mother; and a clean shirt also I want. If you think it proper to come a mile or two on the road to meet me, I shall be very happy to see you, as it will be the only chance you shall have of seeing me for more than a week. My reason for that I shall tell you, which I hope will be next Friday week. I wrote to my mother in preference to you last time, but have left her out this time and thought of you, as I have always done. I cannot say now that I could wish; therefore I shall conclude with hoping that you will attend to what this contains. My best love to you, and remember me to my mother. I am yours affectionately. Josiah Lilly

'Harriet' was found to be twenty-three-year-old Harriet Wright and her body was taken to the Dog and Duck to await the coroner.

Sergeant Brough took the man's hat to Harriet's father, who recognised it as belonging to Josiah Lilly, and so the officers went straight to Josiah's house to find he was asleep in bed. When he was told that they had come to arrest him for Harriet's murder, he exclaimed, 'Good God, is she dead?' and then added, 'If I am to hang, I shall die innocent.' He claimed he had last seen Harriet at 9.30 p.m., but he would later change that time.

He was shown the hat and asked how it had come to be by the canal. 'It was taken off me last night for a trap,' he replied. On arriving at the police station Josiah was taken to a cell, where he was visited by Inspector Edmonds, who he knew. 'Oh Josiah,' Edmonds said. 'How came you to drown the girl?'

'I did not do it, but I am as bad as if I had done so, because I knew she intended to do it.'

Josiah now said that the last time he had seen her was eleven o'clock. They were 'near the brewery,' he said. 'She took my hat and ran towards the canal.' He said she had asked for his handkerchief and when he had refused to give it to her she had grabbed his hat and threw it down at the side of the canal, saying she was going to drown herself.

Reporters attending the inquest described Josiah as a young man of prepossessing appearance, aged about seventeen (in a statement he said he had been born 23 August 1823) with red hair, a fair complexion and an intelligent face.

Witnesses were called who claimed they had seen the couple walking together at nine o'clock on the Wednesday night. Then at 11.30 p.m. Josiah was seen returning 'in great haste' without his hat. The jury viewing the body noticed that her wrists had marks on them as if they had been grasped by strong hands. It wasn't looking good for Josiah as friends also said that he had been getting frustrated with Harriet and had said he would hang for her before the week was out.

Josiah and Harriet had, at one time, been very fond of each other but he had got in with a bad crowd. He had been persuaded by one of these friends to take a day off work without his employer's permission. His master reported him to the police and he was whipped and spent a day in the House of Correction. When Harriet's father found out, he forbade Harriet from seeing him again, but she was too smitten with Josiah and refused to be ruled by her father, so had carried on seeing Josiah without her father's knowledge. They had even decided to get married and had had the banns published. But then Josiah had heard some gossip and felt, as he described, 'her character to be that which I knew would not suit my circumstances.' So he had left Birmingham.

Four months later, however, he changed his mind and returned. Harriet, obviously delighted to see him, persuaded his old employer to take him back and they found furnished lodgings together in Ludgate Hill. But Josiah once again took more time off, this time to spend time with Harriet. His master had him charged and he was sent to the House of Correction again for a further fourteen days. It was during these fourteen days that he wrote the letter found in Harriet's pocket. On being released he found that Harriet had moved back to her father's house.

He hadn't been out long when Harriet's father accused him of stealing some of Harriet's possessions. Whether Josiah had actual stolen them, or whether Harriet had

Cliveland Street is a busy industrial area today. (© V. Morgan)

The canal running from the Walmer Lane bridge at the back of the buildings on Cleveland Street. (© V. Morgan)

just left her bonnet and shawl at the Ludgate Hill lodgings is unclear, but charges were brought against him and the case was due to be heard on Wednesday 5 May. Harriet, however, refused to appear as a witness so the charges were dropped.

Now, just two days later, Josiah had been charged with wilful murder and was awaiting his trial at Warwick.

At the Warwick Summer Assizes on 12 August 1840, Ann Mitchell said she had seen Josiah and Harriet in Cleveland Street, and that later they were seen quarrelling over her bonnet and shawl. Josiah was heard to say that they were at his lodgings and Harriet agreed to go there with him. Another witness said they had seen them walking towards the bridge at 10.30 p.m. Harriet's sister said that Harriet had often said she would 'destroy herself' if Josiah ever turned his back on her.

Mr Daniels, acting for the defence, described Harriet as having a hasty temper and reminded the jury that another witness, Ann Talbot, had said she had seen them together at about ten o'clock, quite happy. He also described how Sergeant Brough had said that Josiah was 'very much hurt and ready to cry.'

The jury consulted for only a short time before finding Josiah not guilty, claiming all the evidence was circumstantial and that, as Harriet had refused to appear against him, the couple were obviously very close.

What happened to Josiah after the trial is a mystery – he disappears from the records.

UNSOLVED

'A young man of respectable appearance'

1844

Suspect:	*William Stanley Warner*
Age:	*Twenty-eight*
Charge:	*Stealing*
Sentence:	*Transportation*

At the time of the 1841 census William Stanley Warner was living at Regent's Parade, Caroline Street, Birmingham. He was aged around twenty-five and was employed as a bank clerk. The 1841 census, not giving a lot of information, just shows that he was living with three female relatives – Hannah Warner, a schoolmistress aged about thirty, Ann Warner, aged about twenty-five, and another Hannah Warner, aged about sixty. One would assume they were related – probably a mother with her three children – and they were affluent enough to have a live-in servant, Caroline Wootten.

William married Hannah Lowe at St Peter and St Paul's in Aston on 27 October 1842 and they went on to have one child. By 1844, William was working as a clerk at the Town and District Bank Company in Colmore Row, Birmingham, earning £80 a year. His salary, like all other employees, was held in a savings account in his own name. He was paid quarterly but was allowed to draw money from the account at any time. In July 1844 it contained £170.

On 26 July, William spent most of that morning working at the back of the office, but just before lunchtime another clerk, Edward Wigner, saw him taking cash and notes from the drawer. There was nothing unusual in this, as clerks were allowed to take cash from the drawer if they required it and, as Edward was engaged with a customer at the time, he made no comment. At one o'clock William left to go to lunch.

When he didn't return from lunch, no one thought anything about it, but as William hadn't asked for the afternoon off, his absence was reported to the manager, Mr Smith. It wasn't until the close of business that it was discovered that a large sum of money

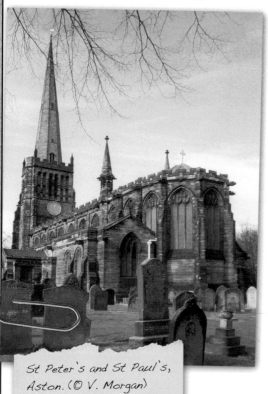

William Warner's entry on the 1841 census.
(HO107/1139/1/30/14. Held in Birmingham Archives and Heritage)

St Peter's and St Paul's, Aston. (© V. Morgan)

was missing. Twelve £100 notes marked 'Birmingham, April 18, 1843' and ten sovereigns had vanished – in their place a receipt from William Warner saying he had taken the wages owed to him.

At first it was thought that all William had done was take his wages and that the rest of the money had been taken by someone else or even just mislaid. Someone was sent to William's house; he was nowhere to be found. After further investigations and questions it was decided that his note was just a smoke-screen for the robbery, and the bank was in no doubt that William Warner was the thief.

Mr Smith contacted Mr Stephens, the head of police, and newspapers reported that 'communications were sent to the different police-offices in the kingdom.' A £100 reward was offered by the directors of the bank for William's apprehension.

William had indeed absconded. It was reported that he had 'engaged a car to convey him about three miles on the West Bromwich road, where he quitted the vehicle, and no further trace of him has yet been obtained.'

Colmore Row in the early 1900s. (Author's collection)

Police Constable Tandy and a fellow bank clerk, Mr Floyd, set off on his tail. They followed him to Shrewsbury, where they discovered that he had spent the night at the Crown Inn, but William had already left town by the time they arrived. Tandy did, however, retrieve William's beaver hat, which he had exchanged for a straw one.

At first it was thought that he had left Shrewsbury and gone to Whitmore railway station to catch a train on the Grand Junction Railway. In fact, William was walking along the Wrexham Road to Chester.

He was easily traced along this route as he had visited every inn along the way. He had become so boisterous that he had been refused lodgings at the latter ones. In fact, the reports stated, 'It would seem he had been drinking constantly from the time he left Birmingham until taken into custody in the state of insensibility.'

William was eventually spotted riding a gig up Watergate Street in Chester in a very drunken state on the Saturday evening. Local policeman, Police Constable Mitchell, thought, for William's own safety, he should be taken to the York Tavern. Here, Mitchell put him to bed and, on emptying his pockets, found nine sovereigns, 14s 10d in silver and 8d in copper in one pocket and, in the other pocket, twelve £5 notes marked Wolverhampton, and eleven £100 notes. Mitchell immediately notified his chief superintendent, Mr Hill, who guessed that he could be the man wanted for robbing the Birmingham bank. When Mitchell looked at the bank notes again, he found that the serial numbers on them corresponded with those on the stolen bank notes.

William Warner was now escorted to the prison but he was so inebriated that he did not appear to know what was happening. It wasn't until he awoke the next morning in his cell that he realised he had been caught.

In the meantime, Police Constable Tandy and Mr Floyd had arrived in Chester and had traced Warner's whereabouts to the York Tavern. Here they heard the story of his arrest and realised they were too late for the £100 reward – Tandy's Chester colleagues had beaten them to it.

William was taken back to Birmingham and stood before Mr Bolton and Mr Beilby, two of the town's magistrates, and was kept on remand. The report in the newspapers described him as a 'young man of respectable appearance,' adding, 'some of his family were in the court and were deeply affected.' It was decided that William had had every right to his wages, so the sum of £170 was deducted from the amount he had stolen. He was charged with having stolen £1,040 from the bank. The wages he took would amount to about £8,000 in modern-day money and the amount he had stolen would be around £70,000.

William appeared at the Warwick Assizes on Thursday, 1 August 1844 and the court was crowded with a large number of respectable people. He himself was said to be 'most respectably attired' and it seemed by his demeanour that he was sorry for what he had done. He pleaded guilty and his defence lawyer, Mr Miller, said he trusted his Lordship would deal mercifully with the prisoner as he was married with a child. He informed the judge that this was William's first offence and that he had previously been of good character. He also reminded him that the pecuniary loss sustained by the bank had been made good.

William, having pleaded guilty, had to wait until the next day to hear his sentence. He was to be transported for a term of fourteen years. The judge said he wouldn't be doing his duty if he did not award a severe sentence where the case involved stealing from one's employers.

On 22 June 1846, William sailed for Australia on the *Maitland*, disembarking at Port Phillip Tasmania sometime at the end of October. He must have been of good conduct as he was recommended for a conditional pardon, and in 1849 he was given a 'ticket of leave'. What happened to him after then remains a mystery. He seems to have dropped the middle name of Stanley and disappeared amongst all the other William Warner's in Australia. There is no record of him returning to England.

His wife Hannah appears on the 1851 census living at Lower Priory with her widowed mother, Sarah, and her brother Edward. She describes herself as 'married' but has no child. Infant deaths were common in those days, and it seems that she lost her child as well as her husband. She too disappears in 1861. Did she also die? Or did she give up on ever seeing her husband again and bigamously remarry? Many did. Or perhaps she found her own way to Australia and joined her husband.

Case Nine

'Oh Frank, what have you done?'

1860

Suspect: Francis Price

Age: About twenty

Charge: Murder

Sentence: Execution

Francis Price was born in Stafford in about 1835. By 1859 both his parents had died and he had lost touch with his brother. Frank, as he was known, had been an apprentice for a shoemaker but had run away and spent a number of years roaming the country working as a runner, liaising between shoemakers and shopkeepers. Sometime in the November or December of 1859 he arrived in Birmingham, intending to travel on to London.

He had some time to spare before his train arrived and so went into the tap-room of the Old Crown, a local public house, to wait. He was served by the landlady's daughter, Sarah Pratt, a girl of about his age, and immediately fell in love with her. So, the London train arrived but left without Frank, who had now decided to stay in Birmingham.

Within a short time Frank and Sarah became sweethearts. They exchanged portraits of each other and by April 1860, Frank had decided to ask her to marry him.

By now, Sarah had moved to the Swan With Two Necks in Deritend, but Frank didn't like the other girls who worked there and, it seems, they didn't like him. They sneered when he gave Sarah presents and spread rumours that Frank was only trying to seduce her – that his intentions weren't honourable. Frank had always found it difficult to mix with other people or to join in their conversations, and this shyness led some people to distrust him. Frank wanted Sarah to end her friendship with one girl in particular who he knew to be a prostitute. He had told Sarah to 'drop her or me'. This resentment led to arguments between the couple and so Sarah broke up with him and gave his portrait back.

On the morning of 16 April 1860 Frank went to see her at work. He wanted Sarah to 'make it up with him' but she wouldn't. He told her that whatever he had was hers, but she said that money wasn't the issue, 'it was the tales'. He asked what harm he had done

The Old Crown, Deritend. Still standing today, it is the oldest inn in Birmingham. (Author's collection)

her and she replied, 'No more than the talk that was about'. When he tried to take her hand she pulled away and went into another room, after which Francis gave up and left.

His only other friend in Birmingham was Henry Evans, a police constable who had known Frank for the three or four months since Frank's arrival in Birmingham. He saw him a couple of days later, on the morning of the 18th, and during their conversation Frank told him he wished he could see Sarah and that he would give anybody five shillings to fetch her for him. Evans left Frank outside Agnes Hone's house at 11 Court 6 House Deritend after suggesting that he might ask Agnes to fetch her.

Agnes was only too willing to oblige and Frank asked her to tell Sarah that her sister wanted her. She set off to the pub whilst Frank waited in her house. Ellen Cain was working in the bar with Sarah when Agnes arrived and she heard her say, 'Your sister wants you at my house. She will not keep you a minute.' Sarah assumed her sister must have left her place, and followed Agnes out of the pub. When they arrived at the house Sarah greeted Frank with, 'Oh, it's you is it?' and Agnes left them alone and went outside to chat to her neighbour, John Powell.

A short while later she heard her puppy cry out as if it had been hurt. 'Surely they are not hurting my dog?' she exclaimed, opening her door. Inside she found Sarah lying on the floor, bleeding heavily. 'For God's sake John,' she said, 'he's done murder.' Frank rushed past her, out of the house and John Powell gave chase, catching up with him after a short distance. Frank stopped and asked, 'What do you follow me for?'

'I suppose you know as well as I do,' replied Powell.

'I've done nothing.'

'Why do you run away then? You may as well give yourself up, for you're bound to be taken.' Frank turned and ran into Bradford Street. Powell spotted Francis Stokes and called to him to help and together they managed to get hold of Frank.

'I've only given her a smack on the nose,' Frank said.

'I hope it's nothing worse,' said Powell. 'But I'm afraid it is. You must come back with me and see.' Frank decided that he would rather go to the police station in Alcester Street and so the three of them set off together. 'Well, she should not listen to talk and then it would not have happened,' Frank grumbled as they

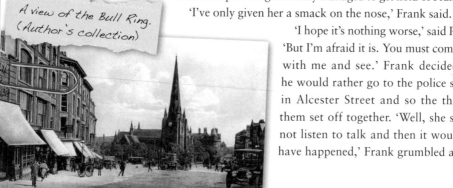

A view of the Bull Ring. (Author's collection)

walked. 'I'm as bad as her, I've listened to tales. Well, what's done can't be undone. I loved her as I loved my life.'

On arriving at the station, Powell explained the situation to the sergeant. A surgeon was immediately sent to the house and Price placed in custody. The surgeon, Mr Jordan, returned to say that Sarah was dead. He described her wounds – there was a deep cut across her throat dividing the large veins and the trachea, and half severing the carotid artery. He said she would have died instantly. Lying at her side was a shoemaker's knife.

When told, Frank seemed surprised. 'Is she dead? It's them women that are the cause of it. I loved her as I loved my life. I know my fate, my days are numbered. I should not care if I was hung tomorrow.' He then took his money from his pocket, which was 35s in total, and asked that it be given to her mother.

'Oh Frank, what have you done?' said Henry Evans when he visited his friend in the cells. Frank claimed he had loved Sarah madly but that he was resigned to his fate. 'I have done it and I know I shall be hung for it.'

Frank said he had asked Sarah to marry him and to leave the place she was working. He had offered her whatever he had and said that it was hers, but she still refused. He had then asked her to take his portrait back, saying he would be satisfied with her just doing that, but she wouldn't. In no statement, or during the court hearing, would he describe what had actually happened in Agnes Hone's house.

When he stood in the dock at the assizes on 4 August 1860, accused of Sarah Pratt's murder, reports said Frank adopted an easy attitude, with hands behind his back, and refused to plead either guilty or not guilty, saying, 'I would rather you would take a verdict for me.'

The defence asked for a verdict of manslaughter, based on the evidence that Frank had desperately wanted reconciliation – in no way did he have murder on his mind when he arranged to meet her. Why would he talk so calmly to a police officer if he was contemplating murder? But the jury didn't agree and found Frank guilty.

His last days were spent taking Bible classes and talking to the prison chaplain, before his execution at Warwick Gaol on 20 August. The hanging was witnessed by a crowd of around 1,500 people and some said Frank hadn't dropped the customary handkerchief to say that he was ready. The hangman, George Smith, appeared to be in a hurry and had withdrawn the bolt without waiting for the signal. At the station an angry crowd assaulted Smith, and the stationmaster, Mr Chiltern, had to lock him in the second-class waiting room for his own safety before he was able to continue on his way to Dudley.

Case Ten

'Oh my wench I wish I hadn't done it'

1861

Suspect:	John Grayson Farquhar
Age:	Unknown
Charge:	Manslaughter
Sentence:	Penal servitude for life

In the early 1800s, Small Heath was a small rural community, but by the middle of the nineteenth century it had developed into an affluent suburb of Birmingham; a place where the upper and middle classes built large houses in order to move away from the bustle of the industrial centre.

At No. 91 Grange Road, Small Health, widower John Grayson Farquhar lived with his nine-year-old daughter, Emily, and a housekeeper, Elizabeth Brookes. John had an annual income of about £400 from the houses he owned which, as a builder, he had no doubt built himself.

John had married Ann Eliza Smith at St Peter and St Paul's in the parish of Aston on 29 June 1847. On the 1851 census they had a one-year-old son, Alex Grayson Farquhar, and John was listed as a 'proprietor of houses'. Alex had died in 1857, followed shortly after by Ann in 1859.

John met Elizabeth Brookes in January 1860. Anyone looking at the 1861 census would think it quite respectable, and expected, that John, a widower and a reasonably wealthy man, would have a housekeeper. But in reality John had become quite attached to Elizabeth and she had become his mistress. She had given birth to his child early in 1861; but it had died soon after birth. By August 1861 they were planning to marry.

On the morning of Thursday, 29 August 1861 John had taken Elizabeth into town to buy her a new dress. Whilst there he had seen her talking with a young man. Whether he was an old acquaintance or just someone being polite is not really known, but it proved to be an unfortunate incident.

On their return, the maid, Martha Phillips, prepared tea and took it into the parlour to them. When tea was finished John asked Martha to go and call for a cab. To fetch a cab was a half-mile round trip on foot. On Martha's return she met John coming out of the door. He told her he wouldn't need the cab now, and walked over to his daughter Emily, who was talking to a neighbour, greengrocer John Penny. Farquhar kissed his little girl and said, 'I have killed Bessy,' and then asked Penny to return to the house with him. Confused, Penny asked what had happened. 'Murder, my God,' was Farquhar's reply.

Meanwhile the maid, Martha, had gone into the house. She went into the parlour and found Elizabeth lying across a chair by the window, her head supported by a cushion resting on another chair at her left side. She had been shot.

John entered the room, followed by Penny, and, looking at Elizabeth, said, 'It was I who shot her. It was I who did the deed.'

Penny sent for the police and Farquhar also asked for a friend, Mr Horsfall, to be fetched. 'Penny, there is a document in that desk which I should like Mr Horsfall to have, respecting my child and property.'

Great Western Arcade; a popular Victorian shopping area. (Author's collection)

At this moment Simon Degge, another neighbour from Muntz Street, arrived having heard of what had happened. 'Oh Mr Farquhar, whatever made you do this?' he asked. John Farquhar put his arms around Degge's neck, buried his head on his shoulder and cried. When he composed himself he knelt down by the body saying, 'Oh my Letty, oh my Letty, why don't you speak to me?'

When John finally got to his feet he had a very wild look in his eyes and picked up a knife from the table. Degge, concerned, asked him to hand the knife over. After an agonising few moments John passed him the knife.

A small part of what remains of Grange Road. Number 61 was further down the road and no longer stands. (© V. Morgan)

When Police Constable Michael Keefe arrived, John was holding Elizabeth and kissing her, saying, 'Bessy why did you tell me what you did? You know I loved you.' Seeing PC Keefe, he said, 'Oh policeman, I have shot her. I am sorry. I give myself up now to you.' He told PC Keefe that he had taken Elizabeth to town to buy a new silk dress and caught her talking to a young man, before saying, 'Her I was determined to marry. I am guilty of murder. It was through jealousy I done it. Please bring the case on as soon as you can for I wish to follow her.'

The inquest into Elizabeth Brookes' death was opened the following Monday morning. John Grayson Farquhar was practically incoherent, constantly repeating, 'Oh my wench I wish I hadn't done it, but she knows I never meant it.' In fact, he became so agitated that the judge eventually requested his removal to another room.

The members of the jury were taken to the house in Grange Road. There they went into the parlour, which was described as a small room lighted at each end by windows. There was a small table in the centre where the tea things from that fateful day were still laid. Elizabeth's body lay on a board, her dress covered in blood that had flowed freely from a large circular wound in the left breast.

Mr Westwood, the surgeon who examined the body, said that it appeared that the gun had been held quite close to her, as the skin around the wound was blackened by gun powder. The abdomen had been penetrated by the shot and the stomach ripped open before it had passed through the liver. Although the maid had said Elizabeth was still alive when she found her, Mr Westwood believed that death would have been instantaneous.

Later that afternoon, Elizabeth was buried at St James' Church, Ashted. The route from Grange Road to Barrack Street, which included Coventry Road, Watery Lane, Lawley Street and Vauxhall Road, was lined with spectators.

Eventually John was able to make a statement. He said that he had ordered the cab as Elizabeth had wanted to go to Saltley to see her family and he hadn't wanted her to go alone. They had had words regarding her having spoken to the young man earlier that day and she had teased him about his jealously. He had picked up the gun in a playful attempt to stop her and she had clasped her hand on his. The gun was unlocked and it had gone off. It was unlocked because earlier John had been showing it to the cabman who had brought them back after their trip into Birmingham.

The defence at John's trial commented on the fact, 'that no one was present as to be able to say how the fatal event occurred which, in the desperate agony of the moment, the prisoner had called murder ... If there were no facts clearly contradicting the account given by the prisoner they could not regard it as an unreasonable one.'

Many witnesses, who had known John for some time, described him as a 'very peaceable, good-natured man', and that he was 'very kind to the poor'. Another neighbour, Margaret Crompton, said of the couple, 'they always seemed comfortable and kind together,' and Martha said that following their return from town that morning, she had only heard words of kindness between them, although John had seemed a little intoxicated.

The jury found John guilty of manslaughter and the judge sentenced him to penal servitude for life, although he seemed disappointed with the verdict, saying, 'It is very fortunate for you that they have found you guilty of the milder offense of manslaughter. I am compelled to lament that I have to pass the lightest sentence of the law in such cases.'

The last we hear of John is a report regarding the execution of two prisoners in Warwick Gaol following their appearance in the same assizes. Prior to the executions, 200 prisoners attended a service in the prison chapel. It was said that during a brief and appropriate exhortation the two condemned prisoners appeared to be much moved, but 'the most emotion was exhibited, however, by the prisoner John Grayson Farquhar who sobbed and moaned audibly.'

What prison he eventually served his prison sentence in has not been discovered, but it seems John may have received a reprieve as he died on 12 December 1866 at No. 84 Coventry Road, of tuberculosis. The fate of his daughter Emily is unknown, as she disappears from the records.

'Will you come back to Sutton now?'

1861

Suspect: John Thompson
Age: Unknown
Charge: Murder
Sentence: Execution

Only a month after Elizabeth's death, in September 1861, the newspapers were reporting that, 'A murder of a particularly shocking character was committed in Birmingham on Sunday afternoon in a house of ill-fame in Tanter Street, well-known as the resort of the lowest characters.'

Ten years earlier, John Thompson would seem to have been living a happy existence with his wife, Eliza, and six children in nearby Sutton Coldfield. He was employed as a 'wire drawer' and later reports would describe him as an industrious and quiet man, who had been employed the greater part of his life and contributed to the support of his mother. But tragedy was to strike over the next decade.

Eliza had died in 1857 and John, like many men in those times, was left to bring up his young children single-handedly.

Not a lot is known about Ann Walker, who also went by the names of Ann Lines and Nancy Dawson, but sometime after the 1861 census was taken (as she is not with the Thompson family then) she went to work for John as his housekeeper, quickly becoming his common-law wife.

Sutton Coldfield. In the nineteenth century it was a quiet village on the borders of Birmingham and in the parish of Aston. (Author's collection)

[or Township] of	City or Municipal Borough of	Municipal Ward of	Parliamentary Borough of	Town of	Hamlet or Tything, &c., of	Ecclesiastical
...ingham	Birmingham	Street Peter	Birmingham	Birmingham		Bishop...

	Road, Street, &c., and No. or Name of House	Houses (In-habited / Un-inhabited)	Name and Surname of each Person	Relation to Head of Family	Condition	Age (Males / Females)	Rank, Profession, or Occupation	Where Born
10	6 Tanter Street	1	Mary Ann Beresford	Head	Un	26	Cap Maker	Warwickshire Birmingham
			Emma do	Sister	Un	24	do	do do
			Selina Lancaster	Lodger	Un	20	Servant	do do
11	do do	1	James Smith	Head	Mar	28	Coffin Furniture Maker	Gloucester
			Elizabeth do	Wife	Mar	22	Silk Weaver	Coventry
12	do do	1	William Walker	Head	Mar	29	Labourer	Warwickshire Birmingham
			Ann do	Wife	Mar	26		do do
			John Williams	Lodger	Mar	30	Mason (Stone)	Bristol
			Sarah do	Wife	Mar	32		do
13	do do	1	Richard Hawkins	Head	Mar	42	Turner	Warwickshire Birmingham
			Ann do	Wife	Mar	40		do do
			Richard do	Son	Un	20	Silver Plater	do do
			Mary do	Dau	Un	18		do do
			James do	Son		12	Iron Polisher	do do
			Eliza do	Dau		6	Scholar	do do
			Ellen do	Dau		3		do do
			John do	Son		2		do do
14	do	1	Sarah Ann Martin	Head	Un	45	Hook Weaver	Liverpool
			Harriet Gridley	Lodger	Mar	33	Boot Binder	Ireland
15	7 do	1	Joseph Ryley	Head	Mar	60	Shoe Maker	Ireland
			Sarah do	Wife	Mar	59	Washerwoman	Staffordshire W...
			Thomas do	Son	Un	10	Lamp maker	do Newark

Households in Tanter Street listed in the 1861 census. Newspaper reports say Ann had been separated from her husband for three years, but is this them living together six months before her murder? (RG9/2146/76/3 Held at Birmingham Archives and Heritage)

Ann had previously been married to a William Walker, who now lived in Manchester. Whether she had left him or whether he had thrown her out is not known, but reports described her as having separated from her husband three years earlier due to her immoral habits. Since then she had lived with several men and supported herself by prostitution.

On Saturday, 28 September 1861, John and Ann went to the Birmingham Fair. They were obviously enjoying themselves as they stayed until gone midnight. At around one or two in the morning they arrived at the door of one of Ann's old lodgings in Tanter Street and asked the owner, Emma Beresford, for a room for the night. Some reports say they were up at eleven for breakfast; others that they were up at 9.30 and went straight out, returning at twelve for about half-an-hour. Whatever happened that morning, it is clear that they were not together by the afternoon, as Ann returned alone at three o'clock, asking if she could lie down. Conversations between her and other members of the house suggested she had met up with a man she used to live with.

When Thompson returned he was told she was resting, and he went to see her. A little later, Emma Beresford went upstairs and noticed their door was open. She could see Ann lying on the bed with Thompson rubbing her arm, which she had hurt in the street, and speaking in kind tones. Emma heard him say, 'Will you go home to Sutton now?' Ann replied, 'Not yet.' When those kind tones turned into raised voices, Emma went up to the attic room again – but by the time she got there everything was quiet.

Emma went back downstairs and sat outside for twenty minutes, but when she returned inside the house she heard Ann scream. Rushing up the stairs, she found Ann, still lying on the bed, but with blood running from a wound in her neck and saying repeatedly, 'I said I would go'. Thompson was standing with his back to the window, holding a knife covered with blood.

Emma ran down the stairs screaming murder and met another of her lodgers, Elizabeth Green. 'Good God, he is killing her,' she cried. Elizabeth rushed to the room in time to witness Thompson pulling Ann from the bed shouting, 'Will you come back to Sutton now?'

Two male lodgers had followed Elizabeth into the room and one later said in court that Thompson appeared quite cool, deliberately cutting the throat of his victim as she lay on the floor.

By now Emma had alerted the police but by the time they arrived, Ann was dead. Dr John Keyworth was called to examine the body. He found two incised wounds on the neck about three inches long. One, across the left side of her throat, had cut through the jugular vein and the other had completely severed the wind pipe. When examined, the knife was found to be an ordinary pocketknife with one blade, the type commonly used by labourers to cut their victuals.

The inquest was held at the Hope & Anchor, Coleshill Street, before the coroner, Dr Birt Davies. A large crowd gathered outside, described by newspapers as 'persons of the very lowest class, a large proportion of them being women'. When the cab arrived carrying Thompson and two police officers, he was greeted with hisses and groans.

He was now described as being pale and nervous, unlike the tough confidence he had displayed when taken into custody. He was charged with murder and taken to Warwick Gaol to await his trial.

At the Warwick Assizes on 16 December 1861, Thompson pleaded not guilty. His counsel, Mr O'Brien, argued that the act had only arisen following a sudden quarrel, therefore justifying a verdict of manslaughter. But the witnesses were all adamant in their statements of seeing Thompson calmly cutting Ann's throat. The jury had no hesitation in returning a verdict of guilty.

Thompson lamented his fate and put it all down to the immoderate use of intoxicating liquors. He said when he went into the room he had no notion of committing murder, he just wanted Ann to go home with him and not stay in Birmingham to meet up with the man she had met earlier. Her drunkenness had upset and she had goaded him. 'In a moment, and without thinking, I cut her throat with my knife. It was done in the heat of the moment, committed while in a state of frenzy brought on by drink and jealousy.'

John Thompson had been tried at the same assizes as Farquhar, who had reserved a lesser sentence, so his sentence caused an outcry. A memorial was sent to the Home Secretary, Sir George Gray, by the mayor and other influential gentlemen, saying that the two cases bore striking similarities and referred to the fact Farquhar was a 'gentleman', thus influencing the sentence:

The execution of Thompson will seriously prejudice the solemn interests of public justice in this town and neighbourhood as the two cases have been generally considered as of similar character, and it is most deeply to be regretted that a painful feeling of uncertainty respecting the administration of the law should be allowed to creep into the public mind.

That your memorialists earnestly entreat that you will take the whole of the facts into your consideration with a view to the commutation of the sentence of death.

A reply was received on 28 December saying that Sir Gray had decided not to recommend Thompson to the 'Royal Mercy'. The execution went ahead on 30 December 1861.

Prior to his hanging Thompson wrote the following, which was later published in the newspapers:

To my fellow brethren I hope my sad fate will be a warning to a great many of both sexes. I little thought that I should come to such an end as this but it is nothing but what I deserve for I am guilty of the deed and very sorry I am. I would soon have undone it if I could. As for the cause I must leave everyone to form his own opinion, for I cannot properly satisfy myself; but you may be sure there was a cause, but it is too long to enter into here. I am sorry I did it for I was very fond of her and she was a clean, good woman in a house.

As for the witnesses, two of them, if not three, committed perjury I am sure – not that it matters to me now, for I know I am guilty, but I do think anybody on oath ought to be very careful and speak the truth, whether any man's life is at stake or not. But I hope God will forgive them as I do myself.

I dare say some will say many hard things of me, but I hope they will be as our Saviour was when they took the woman before him taken in adultery. He said, 'he that is without sin among you let him cast the first stone'. So, I hope, they will treat me. I am not the first and I am afraid I shall not be the last to suffer for the crime of murder, but I hope and trust God will forgive me, as I forgive everyone, and hope that none of my kind friends may come to my untimely end; but this is a wicked and troublesome world to live in.

I conclude with many kind thanks to the governor, chaplain, officers and attendants on me for the kind treatment I have received since I have been in prison and may the Lord God Almighty bless them. Amen. John Thompson.

Case Twelve

'I shook hands and kissed her'

1863

Suspect:	Henry Carter
Age:	Twenty
Charge:	Murder
Sentence:	Execution

The *Birmingham Daily Post* of Tuesday, 7 April 1863 described an event of the previous Easter weekend holiday:

> Going to see a man hanged – to see a fellow creature publicly strangled according to the law! Such was the holiday programme of many who left their beds at an early hour yesterday morning – Easter Monday – and wended their way, either by road, or rail, to the County Gaol at Warwick. The culprit was Henry Carter; his victim was Alice Hinkley, his sweetheart, both of them natives of Birmingham. He was a young man – only just emerging from mere boyhood into man's estate. His sweetheart, Alice, was a pretty well-conducted girl only seventeen years of age, and he, her lover, had now to suffer the issue of that verdict which a jury had pronounced on his crime. Only nine days ago, in the crowded Assize Court, he listened to those impressive words 'that you be taken from the place where you are to the place from whence you came, and there to the place of execution, where you shall be hanged by the neck till your body be dead'.

Alice Hinkley had lived at the back of 110 Bissell Street with her grandmother, close to her parents' own house. She worked for a jewellery maker, Mr Lee, in Essex Street.

Henry Carter was a brass founder who worked for Messrs Whitehouse & Sons and was also an attendant at the Baptist Circus Chapel Sunday School in Bradford Street. He lived at 11 Skinner Lane and had, for five or six years, passed two or three times a day along Bissell Street and so had regularly seen Alice.

Even before Henry had spoken to Alice, he had fallen in love with her. Eventually he asked her father if he could keep company with her, and he was allowed to visit her at home and to walk out with her. They then spent the next eight months courting, but, according to those who knew her, she wasn't really very interested in him. Some said she didn't even seem to like him very much and that during her last weeks she had seemed quiet, which they attributed to a problem with the courtship. However, she hadn't said anything to her parents, even though she had broken off the relationship twice in previous weeks.

Skinner Lane. No houses now, just parking lots. (© V. Morgan)

On the Thursday afternoon of 4 December 1862 Henry had visited Alice's house, only to find that she was out, so had said he would come back in the evening – which he did. After staying in the house until eight o'clock they went out for a walk. Later, her grandmother, Elizabeth Hinkley, came out and found them standing at the bottom of the alleyway. She called Alice in and she said she was coming. Two minutes later Elizabeth heard a gunshot.

Marie Cowrie had walked past Henry and Alice at about 10.40 p.m. and had said to Alice how foolish it was for her to stand there with such a cold as the one she'd got. Alice replied that she hadn't been there long and was just going in. She then heard Carter say, 'Do you mean it?' and her reply of 'Yes'. Marie had walked about thirty yards when she also heard the gunshot. Soon afterwards, Henry Carter ran past her.

Both said in court that they had heard no quarrelling, only low whispers, and the couple's appearance was one of talking on friendly terms. Friends said Henry did have a very impulsive temperament and was very passionate, but they couldn't believe he would do such a thing on purpose.

But now Alice lay dead in the alleyway and a search party was out looking for Henry. He was found two hours later.

Following his discovery that Alice wasn't at home that afternoon, Henry was seen by Samuel Moore looking in a pawnbroker's window. Samuel asked him if he was looking for a watch but Henry said he was looking for a pistol for a friend in the country. Together they walked to a shop in Weaman Street and Henry bought a double-barrelled pistol, some powder and some caps, which he again said was for a friend in the country. He then went to another shop to buy the bullets. Here, Moore warned him that the bullets could 'go through a man', and Henry Hunt, the shopkeeper, told him to be careful where he fired them as they would go a long way and were dangerous.

Carter spent the remainder of his time before visiting Alice in a public house and amused himself by snapping the caps from the gun at a candle. Later, in court, this was referred to as 'practising his aim'.

Henry's trial took place on 28 March. Elizabeth Hinkley, Marie Cowry, Samuel Moore and Henry Hunt were all called as witnesses. The defence admitted death was caused by the prisoner but that it was not necessarily wilful or malicious – there was no motive. They were happy together and if Henry had intended to murder her, would he have gone so openly to buy a gun. They suggested had he just been playing with the gun and it had gone off unexpectedly.

The jury didn't agree and they found him guilty, although they recommended a verdict of mercy as he was only twenty years old.

The judge replied, 'This is not the first of these dreadful cases which has come under my notice in which love has been turned into jealousy and hatred and the object of a man's affections has become the object of his evil passion. The jury have recommended you to mercy, no doubt on account of your age. That recommendation shall be forwarded to Her Majesty's advisors.'

His father prepared an appeal – or 'memorial' as they were called at this time – saying that evidence of insanity had not been brought into the court. Although the proof showed it more as an 'imbecile state of the prisoner's mind' through injuries received at the time of his birth and during childhood. The memorial was to be presented to Sir George Grey on the Tuesday, within the customary fourteen days between trial and execution; however, it was then discovered the execution had been set for the Monday. The authorities claimed that this was quite acceptable as two Sundays would have passed between the trial and the execution. The Mayor of Birmingham, Mr C. Sturge, immediately sent a telegram to Sir George Gray asking for a delay, but the reply came back saying that the law must take its course. A warrant for execution was made out immediately.

Reports stated that Carter was 'only too anxious to pay the last penalty of the law for the awful crime he has committed rather than continue to exist in his present mental trouble'. When asked again if the gun went off accidentally, Henry this time said, 'No. There was no quarrel between us while talking. I shook hands and kissed her before parting and then I shot her. It was through jealously.' Of the motive he said, 'That lies between her and me. None will ever know that.'

He wrote letters to his family and friends all confessing his guilt, saying he had purchased the pistol with the deliberate intent of shooting the girl, that he went to the house on the evening with the express purpose, and that he was actuated to do so through jealousy. On the day before his execution he was not only visited by his own family but also by Mr and Mrs Hinkley. He went down on his knees and asked for forgiveness.

Henry was executed at Warwick Gaol on 6 April 1863 in front of 1,200 people. He attended prayers at ten o'clock and was then led to the scaffold. From here he addressed the crowd below, warning them not to give way to similar feelings lest they should meet a similar fate, which he said he well deserved. He then read a prayer from *The Prisoner's Memorial* before the bolt was removed and the drop fell. Reports said that death was almost instantaneous. Only forty people stayed to watch the body being cut down.

'I loved her intensely'

1864

Suspect: George Hall

Age: Twenty-two

Charge: Murder

Sentence: Execution,
later reprieved

George Hall, a jeweller's stamper aged twenty-two, was described as a steady, peaceable, humane man, and had courted Sarah Ann Smith for several years. They had planned to marry two years previously, but had then quarrelled, after which Sarah was briefly courted by a man named Martin Toy. After a while, however, she had gone back to George and once again agreed to marry him. They had married at St Matthias' Church on Christmas Day 1863.

On her wedding night, Sarah, complaining of a headache, had left her husband and gone back to her parents, William and Jane Smith, at Court 7, Richard's Street, Dartmouth Street. The following morning her mother took her back to her husband but the next day, unknown to George, she visited Martin Toy. During the week that followed she was described as being 'haughty and cross' and did not show any love for her new husband.

On 3 January she went back to her parents permanently. She told her mother 'he has deceived me in saying that he had a home to take me to'. Instead, he had taken her to his sister's house in Farm Street. Sarah was determined that she would not return to him until he had his own house. 'Never mind Sarah,' her mother replied. 'You are both young and strong and he is a steady man; you will soon have a home.'

While back with her parents she took to living the life of a single woman and regularly visited Martin Toy. She was seen with him at the Prince of Wales Theatre by Joseph Flowers, a workmate of George's. A message was sent to George and he arrived in time to see them leaving the theatre.

He later told his master, Mr Simmonds of Hylton Street, that when he had confronted her about the issue, she had declared that she would continue to see Toy. George had then said

Hylton Street in Birmingham's jewellery quarter. The industrial buildings have now been cleaned up for the tourist trade. (© V. Morgan)

that if she was going to carry on in this way then he wanted the things that belonged to him returned. She pulled off her wedding ring and her earrings, thrust them into his hand and then, laughing, slapped him across the face before walking away with Toy.

A week later, Sarah took out a summons against George saying he had threatened her, but in front of the magistrates he told her that he had a perfectly good home for her to return to. She refused and the case was dismissed. Again he confided in Mr Simmonds, saying that he loved her and would do anything for her and that he didn't know she didn't care for him when they were married. 'I am doomed to be miserable for life.'

Sarah continued to live with her parents and Toy regularly visited her there. This caused arguments between her parents and ended with William Smith being arrested on a charge of assaulting his wife, for which he received three months' imprisonment. He appeared in court on 16 February, a day which would end tragically for both George and Sarah's family.

On the night of 16 February, George visited Sarah and sat with her and her mother drinking beer, as he occasionally had in an effort to win her back. They discussed a murder case which had recently taken place in Worcester. Did this give him ideas?

When it was time for him to leave he asked Sarah to put on her bonnet and shawl. He said he wanted her to go with him to fetch something from Constitution Hill, but told her mother he would then bring her back to the top of the street. Sarah thought it might be the earrings, which he said he was going to give her back.

Later that evening, George went into the Wellington Inn and asked for a glass of rum and water. He was noticeably shaking and asked the landlord to join him, saying, 'Perhaps it will be the last time you will have the opportunity.' Asked what he meant, he said that he had just shot his wife on the Dartmouth Street bridge. Friends then accompanied him to his parents' house where he told them what had happened.

'I have told you I would do it and I have done it.'

He said he had bought the pistols, some powder and some bullets at six o'clock that evening in Weaman Street. He handed the pistol over and then sat weeping on the sofa until the police arrived.

When the police constable came to arrest him he said, 'Please don't handcuff me. I've never been handcuffed in my life.' He shook hands with his mother and father and went quietly to the police station.

Sarah was found on the road near the bridge. She had been shot in the cheek and was unable to talk. The bullet had passed through her left cheek, shattering her jaw bone and then settled in a muscle near her spine. The doctor, Mr G. Baker of Ashted Row, said it had 'buried itself beyond reach' and decided it was not worth taking her to hospital. She was taken home where she died the next day, without having been able to say what had happened. Martin Toy had spent an hour and a half sitting by her bed.

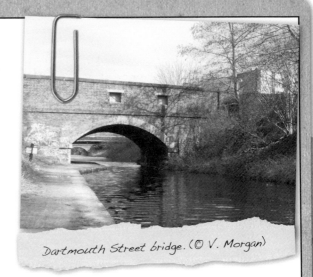

Dartmouth Street bridge. (© V. Morgan)

The jury found George guilty of murder, but recommended mercy on account of the provocation he had endured at his wife's hands. During the trial George had appeared to be in a state of stupor until hearing the verdict – reports described the scene which followed as, 'one of the most distressing scenes that have ever been witnessed in a court of justice.'

He begged to say a few words before he was condemned to die. He said that in all the time he had kept company with her there was no man on earth who loved a girl better, 'and all the time she loved another'. She had wanted a home and said, 'George, if you will give me one chair and a stool I will dwell with you till the day I die.' On the wedding night she had said she did not feel well so wanted to go to her mother. But he found out later that she had spent the night with Martin and she told him, with a sneer, that when she had a child he would not be the father. He said, 'If Martin Toy were here he would not deny what I say about him. I say candidly that Martin Toy has been the ruin of my life that might have been comfortable and happy.'

George asked that his parents and his friends visit him so that they could pray together, and said that when he rose up to the throne of God to be judged, he would be where no man could tear her from him. He then fainted into the arms of the warders. Those in the court were visibly affected and the women in the gallery sobbed loudly. Even the judge appeared moved when passing the death sentence.

Memorials were immediately sent to the Secretary of State, Sir George Grey. Among them was one from a Birmingham businessman, John Skirrow Wright, and Birmingham attorneys, William Morgan and Alfred Fairfax Morgan, but Sir George Grey came to the conclusion that, 'It would be inconsistent with his duty to recommend a commutation of the sentence.' So Revd Canon Miller, together with John Wright, Alfred Wright and William Morgan, went to London to see Sir George Grey in person. Afterwards, William Morgan and John Wright went to Lincoln to see the judge, Mr Justice Byles, who had tried the case. Meanwhile, more affidavits were sent to London. One was even sent from Sarah's mother, Jane Smith, and her grandmother, Jane Witton, which newspapers described as, 'Perhaps the most touching effort yet made to save the life of the convict.'

Every effort was made to bring about a repeal of sentence and eventually at seven o'clock on the Sunday evening, 14 March, the Governor of Warwick Gaol received a reprieve from the Home Secretary. The news was immediately given to George, who was overcome with emotion and could scarcely gasp his acknowledgement.

Just over a week later, in that same newspaper, on Saturday, 19 March 1864, a letter was published verbatim from Jane Smith:

Sir – Will you be kind enough to insert this letter in your daily paper the statements which have been made Respecting the Character of Sarahan Hall are quite incorrect but before i proceed to Correct them allow Me to state the Reason why i did Not Contradict them on the Coroner's inquest the simple Reason is this when i had given evidence i was not allowed to stay in the Room where the inquest was held But was sent out the reason why i did Not Contradict the statements at warwick was because i only went into Court and Gave My Evidence and Came out again i did Not stay to hear the trial the Reason why i have Not publicly Contradicted them through the papers is because i did Not wish to stand in the way of that Mercy to which he was strongly Recommended i had Not the least desire or wish that he should die it is Well Known that i done all in My power to save his life and even Now though he has depraved Me of My Child though he has taken her life away had i the Power i would set him at liberty entirely and freely forgive him.

And Now for the facts he stated at first that she was a long with another Man on Christmas Night. This statement is incorrect Your Reporters will No doubt Remember that I did Contradict this at the Public Office she said on Christmas Night She was unwell and asked her husband George Hall whether he would Consent for her to Go home that Night and under those Circumstances he consented that she Might Go home she left him at about half past 12 o'clock Promising to Return at an early hour on the Saturday Morning she Went at that late hour with Me and her father accompanied by her Cousin Eleanor street and her companion Thomas sheasby these two young People Stayed with her till half past 2 o'clock on them Going home she retired to Bed i am quite sure the only person that slept with her at home was her Grandmother who is 77 years of age to make this statement More Clear one of the neighbours sent her little Girl to My house to see what time it was on the Saturday morning while Sarahan was having her Breakfast the little Girl on seeing her went Back and told her Mother that sarahan was Breakfast with her Mother My neighbour on hearing this Came in to see if there was any truth in what her child had told her and on seeing her Began to chaff and Joke with her in a friendly Manner about her husband.

On the Saturday Morning her father and Me took to her Back to her husband Between 9 and 10 o'clock her father and Me Carried her Box and left her and her Box where they was about to take up their abode at George Halls sisters on saturday Evening they stayed at the old asylum Summer Lane till about 10 o'clock and was accompanied to their lodgings on that Night By Eleanor street and Thomas Sheasby there is One other statement i wish to Correct that is the one Expecting the Child being fathered upon him this be Made before the Judge i Never heard her say anything of the kind.

'He smelt very strongly of creosote'

1868

Suspect:	*Thomas Bagnall*
Age:	*Thirty-two*
Charge:	*Robbery*
Sentence:	*Ten years' penal servitude*

With the coming of the railways many young boys must have dreamt of working on these great iron machines. Thomas Bagnall, a fourteen-year-old farm labourer living with his parents, Walter and Sarah Bagnall in Great Marsh, Penkridge, in 1851, was probably no exception. But with the coming of the railways a new crime also began to make an appearance in which Thomas Bagnall was to play a part. In December 1689, newspapers reported: 'Late on Friday night a robbery, affected by means of the perpetration of an outrage of a particularly daring and still more dastardly character, was committed in the train while proceeding from Edgbaston station.'

By 1861 Thomas had married Eliza and together they had two daughters, Mary, aged three, and Lucy, aged one. They were living along Icknield Port Road, Ladywood, Birmingham and Thomas was working for the London & Western Railway Company and continued to do so for the next eight years.

Early on the morning of 18 December 1869 he set off to his work as a flag man on a ballast train. His train left the steam sheds in Monument Road at 4 a.m. and travelled to Coventry, Rugby and Northampton. It stopped in a siding for about an hour in Northampton and during this time Thomas made a trip into town, to the chemist shop of Samuel Strutt, where he bought some creosote, saying he wanted to cure some bacon. His train started its journey back to Birmingham at 3.30 p.m., arriving back at the sheds at 10.20 p.m. He was last seen by his colleagues at Shepcote Street bridge.

That night, Thomas Carte, who had been employed by the company for twenty-nine years, was working his shift as passenger guard on the Liverpool to Birmingham train. He was also in charge of a cashbox containing £65.

A few yards from the station, towards New Street. (© V. Morgan)

His train left Liverpool at 7.15 p.m. and had arrived in Stafford at 9.55 p.m. Here the cashbox was placed in Thomas Carte's van at the back of the train, in order to hold the cash bags which he was to collect at various stations on the train's journey to Birmingham. The train departed and called at Penkridge, Ettingshall Road, Deritend, Ocker Hill, Princes End, Tipton, Dudley Port, Oldbury, Spon's Lane, Smethwick, Soho before arriving into Edgbaston just before midnight. Thomas Carte collected twenty-one bags in total, the last being given to him at Edgbaston station. The train then left the station on its final stretch to New Street station, just after midnight.

But the train had only travelled 200 or 300 yards when Carte, who was standing writing in his book, heard footsteps behind him. As he turned round he heard a splash and within seconds he realised his face was smothered in a strong-smelling liquid. His face began to burn and he lost his sight and for several minutes afterwards he was blinded. This strong-smelling liquid proved to be creosote. He heard a slight jingling on the step, as if his lamp had toppled over, then silence.

By the time the train arrived at Birmingham New Street, Carte was regaining his sight and could see just enough to know that the cashbox was gone. A search of the train found no sign of the box; the thief must have already jumped off. From the speed the train was going at the time of the theft, it would not have been easy to jump down from it. It was therefore determined that only an employee of the railways could have done it, as only an employee would be accustomed to jumping from a speeding train.

Carte was examined by surgeon Mr Oliver Pemberton, who said that although one eye was badly burnt, he wouldn't lose his sight. It was later reported that despite being in terrible agony for a number of hours, he did eventually recover.

The police said that they were in no doubt that the crime had been committed by someone who knew the company's arrangements. A lid from a breakfast tin used by 'railway servants' was found in the van. The initials 'TB' were on it and it smelled of creosote.

Robert Simpson, the fireman on the train, said that while stopping in Edgbaston he had seen a man walking along the sidings in the direction of the van. He saw the man clearly and was sure it was Thomas Bagnall. He was wearing a billycock hat and the type of coat worn by railway employees.

The cashbox was found broken open on the north siding of Cottage Lane, 175 yards from Edgbaston station. Footprints led away from the railway. Following them through the sleeper fence, the police found themselves in a garden in Shakespeare Street. From there they were led to the sand pits close to Icknield Port Road. It was

New Street station, c. 1906. (Author's collection)

here, the next day, that Peter Pinder of 125 Icknield Port Road, a little further down from Thomas Bagnall's house at 6 Piper's Buildings, found a bag marked 'Princes End No 1' in his pigsty. The pigsty was near the road so it would have been easy for someone to throw something in while passing.

When the police knocked on Bagnall's door at 4.30 in the morning, he looked out of an upstairs window and appeared to be fully dressed. When he answered the door ten minutes later he only wore a shirt and trousers. On entering the house, Detective Cotton spotted a breakfast can on the table. It was missing its lid. When asked why it didn't have a lid, Thomas said he had lost it the day before. Detective Cotton showed him the lid that had been found and he admitted it did look like his. The detective then asked if they could search the house. Thomas said they could and added, 'You will find a little box of money there.' They found £29 10s 7d, which Thomas said belonged to the Platelayers Society of which he was treasurer. Then they found his boots and thought that the nails on them corresponded with the imprints left behind by the perpetrator. Later, a neighbour, Thomas Harris, was to testify that he had seen Thomas walking home at about 12.20 a.m., carrying a bag.

Thomas was arrested although he maintained his innocence. In his cell the police noticed his hands smelt of creosote, particularly the right one. When they commented on this Thomas said it was when Detective Cotton had handed him the lid to look at. When asked how the lid had got into the van, he claimed it must have been 'through larkin'.

Thomas Bagnall appeared at the Police Court on 24 December charged with stealing the cashbox containing £65 5s 8d and assaulting the guard. Witnesses included Samuel Strutt, the chemist, who said he recognised Bagnall not only by his features, but also by his cap and smock as well. When police had searched Bagnall's

Hagley Road, Edgbaston, c. 1900. A left turn would take you up to Icknield Port Road and the station. (Author's collection)

house they hadn't seen any ham there waiting to be cured. Bagnall insisted he had bought the creosote for someone else, who, knowing the creosote was better at this particular shop in Northampton, and knowing that the train was going there, had asked Thomas to get some for him.

Princes End stationmaster, John Johnson, said that he had noticed in his bag of money a sixpence which had had an uneven edge. Being shown the money which had been found at Thomas' house, he picked out this sixpence.

Other witnesses who worked with Thomas admitted that he was an expert at getting in and out of moving trains. He had achieved this feat with no trouble, even if the train was going at fifteen or twenty miles an hour.

Thomas was charged to appear at Warwick Assizes on Saturday, 27 February 1869, where he was found guilty. The judge, Mr Justice Hayes, in sentencing Thomas Bagnall to ten years penal servitude, said he had not 'for a long time met with a case of crime characterised by such wicked daring both in its plan and its execution.'

The 1871 census shows Thomas in the Portland Convict Establishment in Dorset. His wife is still in Icknield Port Road, at number 6 Piper's Buildings.

Thomas served his sentence and returned to his wife and they had another child, a son named John, in October 1880. The family then moved to Idle in Yorkshire where, unbelievably, Thomas got himself a job back on the railways. The 1881 census shows his occupation as 'railway sub-inspector'. Ten years later he is a railway inspector. He died in 1912.

Case Fifteen

'It's me who chived him, see feel the knife, it's wet'

1875

Suspect:	*Jeremiah Corkery*
Age:	*Twenty*
Charge:	*Murder*
Sentence:	*Execution*

'This is one of those cases which display a state of lawlessness and rioting in Birmingham of a very unusual and serious character.' This is how newspapers described the following case, which saw one man tried for murder and seven men tried for assaulting police officers in the execution of their duties, with intent to prevent the apprehension of a man wanted for burglary. The incident happened in what was described as 'the roughest part of Birmingham.' All those charged pleaded not guilty. Mr Adams QC, opening for the prosecution, said that, 'Lately a spirit of insubordination had arisen among a certain class in Birmingham and such outrages had become frequent.'

On 6 March 1875, a 'free and easy' had been organised at the Bull's Head, Fordrough Street in Birmingham. This type of music hall was quite popular in pubs at that time. During the course of the evening, when everyone was busy watching the entertainment, a robbery took place. The following evening, a young girl who had witnessed the robbery, spotted one of the culprits sitting back in that very same public house, drinking with his friends. The police were immediately informed and arrived to arrest William Downes.

There were about twenty people in the room at the time and they were already quite intoxicated and making a lot of noise. As Detective Fletcher and Detective Goodman took Downes, someone shouted, 'They're taking Billy,' and a group followed them out into the street. In no time at all others had joined them and they started throwing stones. The crowd was estimated as being anything between fifty and a hundred.

The detectives asked Sergeant Fletcher and Police Constable William Lines to keep the mob back; during the course of this, Lines found it necessary to chase after a couple of men who ran off. When he returned he found Fletcher on the ground being assaulted

Navigation Street today. (© V. Morgan)

by two men. One of these was Jeremiah Corkery. Lines struck him with his staff and Corkery was seen to strike the police constable near the ear in retaliation. Moments later, blood was oozing from Lines' ear and witnesses heard him cry out, 'Oh no, I shall die!' It transpired that he had been stabbed and twenty-year-old Jeremiah Corkery was found to have been carrying a knife.

In hospital, William Lines said he couldn't be sure who it was who had stabbed him but he had managed to strike the assailant with his staff. The next day, Corkery was bragging about his black eye. Several witnesses saw Corkery strike William Lines. One said he saw Corkery pull a knife out of his pocket and run up to Lines. Another that he had heard Corkery say afterwards, 'It's me that chived him, see feel the knife, it's wet.' To another he said, 'I got it hot, but I served him out.'

Police Constable William Lines died seventeen days later. He had worked the Navigation Street and Fordrough Street area for some time and was well-known by the locals.

His statement told how he had been on duty in the area and had seen the detectives bring Downes out of Fordrough Street and into Navigation Street. They had been followed by a lot of men. One he recognised as Aaron Rogers and he heard him say 'Come along, you'd let any poor ******* get took.' Lines placed himself between the detectives and the crowd.

He said another two he recognised were Thomas Whalen and John Cresswell. Rogers now shouted, 'We want to get you by yourself you ✱✱✱✱✱✱✱ pig.' The mob now started throwing stones and Lines backed down to the White Lion. The three men rushed past him and he chased them around the corner into Suffolk Street, where he saw them knock Fletcher to the ground. A fourth man, who he didn't know, had now joined them and they turned on Lines. He said he knew instantly he had been stabbed, but he couldn't say which one had stabbed him.

The case was heard at the Warwick Assizes on 7 July 1875, and the judge's instructions to the jury were two-fold: was it definitely Corkery who struck the fatal blow and, if so, then had Lines exceeded in his duty? If that was the case then the verdict should be manslaughter and not murder. But he added, 'it would be impossible for those to whom the keeping of the public peace was necessarily entrusted to, to preserve order if they did not act with firmness. When one constable was being kicked upon the ground a constable would be neglecting his duty if he did not use his staff.' He pointed out that Corkery knew that Lines was a police officer and that he was in the execution of his duty.

Jeremiah Corkery was found guilty of murder and sentenced to death. Aaron Rogers and Samuel McNally were acquitted of wounding with intent of causing grievous bodily harm. William Kelly was also acquitted of the same charge but received five years' imprisonment for assault on a police officer in execution of his duty. Thomas Leonard, Charles Mee, John Cresswell and Thomas Whalen were all given life imprisonment for that same offence. William Downes received five years for burglary.

On passing the sentences, the judge said he thought the jury were fully justified in the conclusion at which they had arrived. Jeremiah Corkery then addressed the jury:

The corner of Suffolk Street and Navigation Street. (© V. Morgan)

Gentlemen of the Jury I wish to say a few words if you will be kind enough to listen to them. It is not anything that I care about saying. I don't wish for any pardon or mercy, but simply to say that it looks like common sense that if a man was struck by another man that man would know who struck him again. I hope to put it before you and say a little word which I think it only proper I should say, and that is that you can see perfectly plain that I am here innocent of this charge. Not that I wish to gain mercy or anything of that kind but you can see there is a plot to put me into this case to get other people out. The verdict is passed and it is no good me saying anything against it, but I wish now to leave it all in somebody else's hands – the Judge of all judges.

While waiting for his execution Corkery had few visits from his family, apparently at his own request. But he did tell those who did visit him that, despite what he had said in court, he had stabbed William Lines.

He was executed in the precincts of Warwick Gaol on 27 July 1875 at eight o'clock in the morning and, for all his previous bravado, it seems his last few hours were spent 'tossing in a troubled manner and evincing much mental suffering'. The report went on to say that on his short walk to the gallows, 'he trembled violently and his knees occasionally gave way'. He kept his head bent so low, that the executioner had difficulty in placing the noose around his neck, and just before the final drop he 'expressed his deep sorrow that he had been guilty of a fearful offence, and humbly implored mercy'.

Jeremiah had already spent six months in prison after being convicted of larceny in April 1872. Twelve months later he had been tried again and received another twelve months, with one year's police supervision. Now, as his body hung from the end of a noose, he received no sympathy from the newspaper reporters: 'Thus passed away Jeremiah Corkery, who was guilty of a fearful crime, and who amply merited its terrible punishment.'

William Downes went on to attempt other burglaries. On 20 April 1881, he received five years' penal servitude followed by seven years' police supervision for 'possession of house breaking implements [by night] after a previous conviction'.

For the four who received life, they were sent to serve their sentence in Gillingham in Kent, where they are found on the 1881 census.

Following this tragedy, and coupled with other circumstances, Joseph Chamberlain, then Mayor of Birmingham, fought to have the slum streets of Birmingham cleared and improved. Land was bought by the council and a new road, Corporation Street, was built to make a more direct route through the town.

Case Sixteen

'I've just thrown old Paget's daughter in the canal'

1879

Suspect: John Ralph

Age: Twenty-eight

Charge: Murder

Sentence: Execution

Alice Paget (also known as Sarah Alice) was only eighteen years old when she married Henry Vernon, a jeweller, at St Mark's Church, Birmingham on 24 September 1870. The marriage proved an unhappy one and nine years later, on 31 May 1879, she was found in the canal, with her throat cut. But this wasn't the act of a jealous husband; it was the act of a rejected lover.

Alice lived with her husband in Brighton Place, Shakespeare Road, and they had one child who was aged about five years old. They had only recently moved there from No. 72 Summer Hill Street.

John Ralph, a basket maker and hawker, was twenty-eight and lived along Heath Street South. He was married but lived separately from his wife. He had met Alice sometime around Christmas and an affair quickly began, though there are conflicting reports as to whether it was Ralph who was infatuated with her or she with him.

Alice's servant, sixteen-year-old Hannah White, gave evidence as to the intimate relationship between Alice and John Ralph. They had been seen together constantly during those six months, often drinking in local public houses. But it seemed this relationship was coming to an end. Friends said that Alice was becoming bored with John, and John seemed to have taken this badly. Hannah also said that the week before the murder he had snatched Alice's purse and Hannah had had to help retrieve it. Then she saw John hit her mistress.

A friend, Rachel Parton, had also witnessed John Ralph strike Alice Vernon, but it had seemed in a jokey way and she had slapped him back. Maria Carter had also seen them quarrel and had heard John accuse Alice of going with other men. He would often laugh and say, 'Well I ain't the only one!' Alice had also told her she wanted to end the relationship, saying once when she saw him walking towards her, 'Look there, I want to get rid of that ******, but I cannot.'

On Friday evening, 30 May, Alice had taken tea and then told her child that she wouldn't be home that night as she was going to Erdington. At 6.45 p.m. she had gone to Eliza Moreton's house in Whitmore Street, Hockley, and the two of them had decided to go for a drink. They met John Ralph waiting in the street, so the three of them had gone to the Welcome public house, where they each had a jug of ale. They laughed and joked together and Eliza said that Alice and John had playfully tapped each other on the cheeks. Then John had told Alice he was going away for three weeks and would leave her a mark to remember him by. She had said, 'Don't do that; give me a kiss.'

They left the Welcome and John left the two ladies on their own so they decided to take a walk. Alice now told Eliza that she had tired of Ralph and wanted to be rid of him. A little while later, when they spotted John, Alice pulled Eliza into The Tram public house in an effort to avoid him. But John began jumping up at the window and when he spotted them, went in. They left at 9.45 p.m. and Eliza went her separate way, but she said the couple appeared quite friendly and perfectly sober walking down Icknield Street when she left.

Later, at about 10.30, Ralph went into another public house, the Why Not. He ordered a glass of water and asked to borrow a sharp knife. Elizabeth Payne, the landlord's wife, asked him what he wanted it for. He said he needed to mend some twigs on a basket.

During that evening a cabman, William Harborne, said he had seen Alice Vernon in the company of a man, who he did not know, on the canal bridge on Spring Hill at about 11.30 p.m. George Robertson, a general dealer of 91 Spring Hill, whose windows looked out over the canal, heard his dog barking at about 12.40 a.m. Looking out of his window to see what was happening, he heard a loud scream coming from the banks and a woman's voice cry out, 'Oh don't!' twice. He threw open the window and shouted, 'What's up?' but heard no reply.

At three o'clock in the morning Police Constable George Benton was patrolling the area around Springhill when John Ralph came up to him and said, 'I've just thrown old Paget's daughter in the canal.' Benton hesitated, not quite realising what he had heard, so Ralph continued. 'Here I am, put them on me.'

'What on you?' Benton asked.

'The handcuffs.'

'What for?'

'For shoving a woman into the water. There she is.'

Ralph pointed to the water where a body could clearly be seen floating on the surface. As Benton secured Ralph he called for assistance and two other police officers quickly arrived. They went down to the canal to retrieve the body. As they were about to take the body out of the water Ralph said, 'Take me away, I do not want to see it.'

The surgeon, Mr Burton, examined the body. There were three incised wounds in the throat, deep wounds on the first three fingers of the left hand and on the third finger of the right hand, a contusion on the head and on the left cheek: three slight wounds in the back of the neck and three deeper wounds extending from the side of her neck to the front of the throat. The external jugular vein was divided and the internal jugular was penetrated. However, in his opinion these wounds would not have caused her death and they would have been treatable. Her death was caused by drowning.

When Constable Benton took John Ralph to the station he said, 'I did push her into the canal and when she attempted to get out I pushed her in again.' But he denied cutting her throat, although he admitted that they did have a knife to cut some bread and cheese, 'so she may have cut herself in the struggle.' The surgeon also examined his hands and found a wound which could have been caused by a fingernail.

It was her father, Thomas Paget, a zinc worker of 72 Summer Hill Street, who identified Alice's body. So what had happened to her husband? He seems to have played no part in the proceedings and is not mentioned in any reports as attending the inquest or assizes. The couple had lived in Brighton Place for only a week prior to Alice's murder and her servant, Hannah White, said she often spent the night away from home. Hannah had been told by Alice not to say anything to Mr Vernon.

At the inquest at the Public Office, Ralph was described as paying 'great attention to the evidence'. He appeared to be perfectly calm throughout the whole of the proceedings. But when the trial took place on 5 August 1879, the defence's only case was that there was no evidence of premeditation.

John Ralph was found guilty of murder, and, in pronouncing the death sentence, the judge said he held no hopes for reprieve.

He was executed at Warwick on 26 August 1879.

Since the new law of ten years previous, which had brought about private hangings, it was now usual in some parts of the country for reporters to be excluded from witnessing an execution. However, the High-Sheriff of Warwick thought it still advisable for independent witnesses to be present, to make sure that the execution had been carried out properly, so a reporter was allowed in.

The bell began to toll in Warwick Gaol at eight o'clock but reports said it was so windy that it could hardly be heard. The yard door opened and the governor, under-sheriff, prison surgeon and prison chaplain appeared, followed by John Ralph and two wardens. The chaplain began reading the first few sentences of the burial service – a customary occurrence then, even though the prisoner wasn't yet dead. Ralph was not heard to make any response but kept a calm demeanour and appeared fully resigned to his fate. He walked with his head held high but was deathly pale. His legs were tied and the white hood placed over his head, followed shortly after by the noose. Then the lever was pulled. Death was almost instantaneous.

'Her head was battered in'

1888

Suspect:	*George Nicholson*
Age:	*Fifty-three*
Charge:	*Murder*
Sentence:	*Execution*

In 1881, a crime took place which the newspapers reported as being made up with all the familiar elements – intemperate habits, a loss of position in life as a result, an unfortunate marriage and quarrels over money matters.

George Nicholson was known by the locals as 'Old Cuckoo'. He was originally from Kineton in Warwickshire and at one time had lived in Walsall, but most of his life had been spent in the Birmingham area.

He was a baker and had moved around quite a bit and had already been married three times. At one time he had been a master baker with his own shops. Over the years these had been in Ward Street in Birmingham, Tower Street in Aston and Rupert Street in Nechells. In 1881 he had bought an out-door beer license for a property in Clissold Street, Birmingham. In 1856 he married Ann Davis and they had had a son, Francis, in 1857. They were listed as living in Camden Street on the 1861 census and had a shop in Norton Street, Balsall Heath on the 1871 census. Ann died in 1874 and a year later George married Margaret MacLennan. She died in the summer of 1882 and in February 1883 he married Mary Ann Ecclestone. Fifty-two-year-old Mary was a widow and had several children from her first marriage; some of whom lived with Mary and George after their marriage. George's own son was now a baker himself and living in Shropshire.

What his other marriages had been like no one knows, but his third marriage proved to be an unhappy one. By now he was said to have become 'unsteady' and his business began to slip away. He was forced to become a 'journeyman' and find work wherever he could. In September 1888 he had been working for Mr Taylor, a baker in Gower Street, for six weeks.

The Barton Arms. (Author's Collection)

George and Mary were now living at 27 Burlington Street, Aston. Mary worked as a mangler and because she paid the rent, she charged George board and lodgings. On 22 September 1888 she went out shopping with her daughter. On their return later that afternoon, they found George at home. He appeared to have been drinking, although he didn't seem drunk, just in a bad mood. He said he had been in the Barton Arms in Newtown Row after work.

Mary's daughter went home and said later that at that time she thought they seemed to be on friendly terms. But only a short while after she had left, their neighbour, Mrs Martha Wark, heard the couple quarrelling about money. She could hear George shouting, 'Look, I've given you 1s 6d' and Mary answering, 'That won't do. I need 2s.' Then the voices suddenly stopped and Martha heard what she described as the sound of a chair being turned over.

George was seen to leave the house by the back door.

At ten o'clock Mary's son and daughter, Albert James and Prudence, arrived home and saw their mother sitting in her rocking chair by the fire. But she seemed to be breathing heavily and didn't answer when they called to her. Then they realised she was unconscious, and that 'her head was battered in, her brains protruding, and she was covered in blood.'

Albert rushed out for a doctor and Prudence followed him outside. Police Constable Russell found her out on the street crying, 'He has killed my mother.' He rushed into the house with Prudence just as, as his statement says, Mary breathed her last. Dr Vincent Jones of Asylum Road arrived shortly afterwards and confirmed she was dead.

There were three wounds on the top of her head, from ear to ear, which would have been made by a sharp instrument used with great force. Her chair, the carpet and hearth rug were saturated in blood.

In the scullery Superintendent Walker and Detective Inspector Winkless found a heavy coal hatchet covered with clots of blood and hair. It was a type typically found in a house of that class – sharpened at one end for chopping wood and flattened at the other for breaking coal.

Her children noticed that the silver watch and gold chain Mary normally wore were missing.

Descriptions of George were quickly despatched to neighbouring authorities. He was aged fifty-three, five feet six inches in height with a pale, thin face and dark whiskers. He had a humped-back, so was described as being 'deformed'.

On leaving the house, George had been met by Mrs Wark's husband, but nothing showed in George's manner that there was anything wrong. He then went to Newtown Row and the pawnbroker, Mr Rubenstein, where he gave his name as George Harris of Park Lane. Here he pawned the watch and chain for 23s. He was then seen boarding the 10.55 train to Walsall. Police searched all the boarding houses in Walsall, but he hadn't been seen at any of them. He was eventually spotted by Sergeant Edward Marshall, walking along Park Street in what was described as a casual way.

When Marshall approached him he said, 'Hello George,' and George replied, 'George what?'

'George Nicholson of course,' was the answer. But George said there must be some mistake as his name was Jones. On being arrested he still maintained he wasn't their man, but the pawn ticket was found in his pocket, his coat sleeve was smeared with blood and there were spots of blood on other parts of his clothing. He was taken back to Birmingham by Sergeant Parker, all the time showing an appearance of indifference and unconcern, and keeping up the pretence and denial of murder.

At the police station in Birmingham he made no statement apart from denying his name was George Nicholson, but his stepchildren confirmed it was him. When charged he said, 'Oh, very good. She is dead is she? You say I killed her?' The charge was repeated and he said, 'I know nothing about it. My name is not Nicholson and you have no business to bring me here. I had a lot to drink last night and I was very drunk.'

A fellow worker at Mr Taylor's, Harry Townsend, said George had been acting strangely for a few days. He had even said he would make a 'Whitechapel job of his wife.'

At Warwick Assizes on Monday, 17 December 1888, Mr Soden, counsel for the defence, called for a verdict of manslaughter. He pleaded that there had been no premeditation or preparation for the crime, and argued that it was natural that the children would side with their mother in blaming him for the arguments. But the judge said that no amount of quarrelling or words should reduce the crime to manslaughter. The jury took six minutes to find George guilty, but even then he still kept protesting his innocence.

George Nicholson was executed in Warwick Gaol on 8 January 1889. Prior to this he had only been visited by his stepson. At the execution a man in the crowd outside the gaol said he knew George well and that he had been too fond of drinking and lounging about. Within a minute of the execution the press were allowed in to view the body, the law now having been changed to exclude them from actually witnessing an execution. They wrote:

> The body was hanging still, the rope having been steadied by the hangman. Nicholson's head was leaning on one side and his shoulders seemed bent, giving the appearance of a curvature of the spine. The fingers were unclenched and the doctor was holding one wrist of the dead man in one hand and his watch in the other. Slight twitches of the head were noticeable. In less than two minutes the doctor replaced his watch in his pocket and left the body. He declined, however, to say how long the pulse beat.

Afterwards, the prison governor made a statement to the reporters, saying that George had fully acknowledged the justice of his punishment, confessed his guilt and forgave everybody. He died in the hopes of heaven and of having made his peace with God. He ended by saying that George 'wished this to be made known.'

SOLVED

Case Eighteen

The Daring Street Robbery in Birmingham

1891

Suspects: James Webb, Thomas Wood and William Cutler

Ages: Twenty to Twenty-three

Charges: Robbery

Sentences: Six months to five years' imprisonment

'When it is stated that thousands of pounds are carried through the streets to and from the various banks every day, and particularly on Saturdays which is pay-day at the shops and factories, it is at any rate a compliment to the police force to say that this is the first robbery of the kind that has been committed.' So began a newspaper report in March 1891.

It was said that Thomas Fallon and Thomas Wood had gone to school together, but around ten years later, in 1891, they were to meet again in very different circumstances. That meeting would appear under a newspaper headline, 'The Daring Street Robbery in Birmingham'.

By now, Thomas Fallon was a young man of eighteen. He lived in Meriden Street with his Irish mother, Elizabeth, and younger sisters, Jane and Louisa. His occupation on the census is given as 'merchant's clerk'. Thomas Wood was a tube-drawer and lived on Cheapside, but he had also taken up a life of crime and had been convicted on a number of occasions.

On Friday, 20 March 1891, thieves broke into a warehouse belonging to Martin Flynn, a printer, at 6 Albert Street and stole the safe. As well as containing cash amounting to £8, the safe also held a silver watch and various books and papers. Later that same night, witnesses saw men pushing a heavily laden barrow along Fazeley Street, heading for the canal. Then they heard a splash of water and the men were seen returning with the empty barrow. One of these men, James Webb, was recognised by one of the witnesses. On seeing his acquaintance, Webb laughed and said, 'It's taken a long time to kill a cat.'

When these witnesses heard about the break-in at the printers they informed the police, who searched the canal and fished the safe out of the water. It had been broken open and the money and watch were missing, but the books and papers were still inside the water-logged compartment.

No doubt Thomas Fallon had also heard of this burglary. Perhaps they had talked about it at Henry Bisseker's, a brass chandelier manufacturers in

Fazeley Street canal. (© V. Morgan)

New Bartholomew Street, where he worked. But nearly a week later he had probably forgotten all about it and, without a thought, left his office to collect the wages from the bank. As it was Easter that coming weekend the wages were being drawn a day early, due to the Friday being Good Friday. So, at four o'clock on Thursday 26 March Thomas Fallon went off to Lloyds Bank at Temple Row to collect the weekly wages, together with another clerk, Mary Higginson. Mary used to go on her own but a few months earlier something had happened (exactly what, we are not told) which made her think that an attempt had been made to grab the wages. Following that, Thomas Fallon had accompanied her, carrying the money bags.

At the bank they were given bags of gold, silver and copper amounting to £157 and, with the money hidden in a satchel, began making the return journey back to their employers, taking their usual route along Union Street, Albert Street, Moor Street into Paternoster Row. They got as far as the corner of Paternoster Row and Bordesley Street when a man rushed out from a passage and pushed in between them. He hit Thomas across the side of the head, snatched the bag and ran down Bordesley Street. Fortunately

Thomas wasn't hurt so was able to run after him down Bordesley Street, catching up with him on the corner of Allison Street. He grabbed him but the man turned sharply and gave Thomas a punch on the face, forcing him to let go. The thief ran down Coventry Street into Railway Terrace and a passageway leading into the opening of a one of the many courts in the area. It was here that Thomas lost sight of him.

Temple Row. (© V. Morgan)

An aerial view of St Philip's Cathedral, showing the buildings and roof tops of the surrounding Temple Row and Colmore Row. (Author's collection)

The empty satchel was later found in the outhouse of a property in Allison Street. Neither Thomas nor Mary Higginson recognised the man, and neither of them saw his face clearly enough to describe him, but both could remember what the villain was wearing – a blue coat and light trousers with a heavy blue muffler around his neck.

Superintendent Black and his men began the investigation and they soon realised that the two thefts were connected and the work of a local gang.

On the Saturday morning six police officers were sent to make arrests, and they succeeded in arresting three men for the theft of the safe: John Hannen, a polisher from Bordesley Street; William Clarke, a brass dresser also from Bordesley Street and James Webb a brass dresser from Coleshill Street. William Butler, a labourer of Lancaster Street, and Thomas Fallen's old school companion, Thomas Wood, were arrested for the street robbery. James Webb was charged with both offences.

The newspaper made the comment, 'All the men, whose ages range from twenty to twenty-three, are well-known characters.' Wood was also said to have made the comment that he would have willingly done eighteen months for his share of the money.

Later that day, police detectives went to a house in Ryder Street where James Kelly lived. His daughter was known to cohabit with James Webb. When searching the Kelly's house the detectives found £16 in gold and £2 10s in silver, hidden under the bed, and another 10s wrapped in some paper. While they were searching, Kelly's daughter came into the house and was heard to ask her father, 'Have they found it yet?' She later denied ever saying this. But neither Kelly nor his daughter could account for how they had come into possession of these coins, so were arrested for knowingly receiving stolen goods.

William Butler had been arrested in a local public house while sitting next to a William Cutler. But had the police made a mistake owing to the similarity in names? Later in the cells, Wood and Webb were heard to tell Butler that they knew he was innocent and would 'see him all right'. Wood said it was Cutler who had snatched the bag and he had run after him, to see 'if I could get my corner'. So a deal was struck between William Butler and Superintendent Black and Butler was released. Police then arrested William Cutler.

At the Birmingham Police Court on Thursday 9 April, James and Mary Kelly were discharged due to insufficient evidence, but Wood, Webb and Cutler were charged to appear at the Quarter Sessions the following week.

On seeing Cutler, Mary Higginson now said she was sure it was him she had seen snatch the bag. Another witness, passer-by Joseph Smith, said he thought it was Webb. John Morris said he had seen Webb and Wood together near where the robbery took place and around that time. Thomas Reynolds said he had seen them both running away just afterwards. One of them had something bulky under his coat.

William Clarke (eighteen), together with James Webb (twenty), was also charged with breaking into the warehouse. Clarke said he had only been helping his friend push the barrow – he hadn't known what was in it. Clarke was sentenced to six months but Webb's sentence was deferred to await the outcome of the robbery trial.

He now joined Thomas Wood and William Cutler on the robbery charge.

William Butler, who had been released, now gave evidence. He said he had been in a cell with the others and that Wood had said, 'Cutler was the man who snatched the bag.' He said he had only been sitting next to Cutler in the public house where he was arrested.

The men received various sentences from six to eighteen months. James Webb receiving eighteen months due to previous convictions and the ring leader, Thomas Wood, received five years.

Perhaps an amusing anecdote, which would not have happened in this day and age, was that during the hearing some of the lights went out and others were described as just 'a glimmer'. The hearing was stopped until candles were brought in and then the proceedings continued.

Case Nineteen

'I was there but I don't know what I did'

1893

Suspect: John Thomas Cherry

Age: Nineteen

Charge: Murder

Sentence: Five years' penal servitud

The *Birmingham Daily Post* published on 25 December 1893 (you could still get your local newspaper on Christmas Day in those days) read:

> For the past few weeks Birmingham has been fairly free from serious cases of assaults with the knife. In the earlier part of the year there was quite an epidemic of this class of violence and the Recorder of Sessions and Judges of Assize rightly deemed it necessary to pass some exemplary sentences on offenders found guilty of unlawful wounding. These warnings seem to have had their effect, with the result that, for the time at any rate, offences in which the use of the knife has played a dangerous part have occupied a less conspicuous place on our criminal records.

The report went on to say that on the evening of Saturday 23rd, a man was stabbed to death in Digbeth, 'when the street was crowded, yet so quickly did the assailant give the fatal blow that no one appears to have noticed him, and he succeeded in making his escape. Nothing seems to be known of the occurrence except that a scuffle was heard, and the deceased was seen to fall.'

On another page of the Christmas Day issue, a report told of the build-up to Christmas but added:

> Unfortunately the eve of the Christmas holiday is usually prolific in offences which are far too serious to be overlooked, and the staff of our hospitals can bear testimony to the many acts of violence which are the outcome so often of over indulgence on these

occasions. In addition to the terrible tragedy in Digbeth there were many who sought the skill of the surgeons at the hospitals for more or less serious wounds received in the course of drunken squabbles or at the hands of violent men and women. This seamy side of our city life, however, is not one to emphasis unnecessarily.

In 1891, John Metcalf was a labourer at the gas works and living at 49 Bracebridge Street with his parents, John and Elizabeth Metcalf, his brother Joshua and sister, Emma.

Two years later, twenty-two-year-old John was still living in Bracebridge Street, and on this particular evening had met a friend by the name of Davis and gone to the Pavilion Music Hall. Here they had a couple of pints and left, perhaps to go elsewhere. When they got outside Metcalf told Davis that he was just going across the road and would be back in a minute. But he never went back.

Witnesses said that they had heard a scuffle and then saw a man lying in the road. Thinking he was just drunk, they went to help him up, but he didn't move. Then they saw blood on the road and found it was flowing from a wound in the man's neck behind his right ear. They took him to Mr Keeling's fishing tackle shop and sent for a doctor. But as soon as the wound was plugged, blood gushed from his mouth and the doctor realised it was because the carotid artery had been completely severed.

John Meltcalf gradually bled to death.

Detectives spent all of Christmas Eve making enquiries and it soon became clear that there were many versions to the story, and it was reported that the police were said to be treating some of the informers as suspicious. Reports said there was 'an air of mystery about the whole matter' and that detectives were finding the evidence hard to unravel.

The Metcalf family listed on the 1891 census.
(RG12/2419/74/9. Held in Birmingham Archives and Heritage)

But a couple of days later it was suggested that, although detectives were struggling under all the conflicting statements which were being given, it was felt that an important arrest would be made within a few days. Indeed, that day, at the Victoria Law Courts, five youths were charged. They were William Fallon (sixteen), a bricklayer's labourer of 10 Court 3 House, Communication Row; John Cherry (nineteen), nail maker of back 77 Cox Street West; Freeman Keele (eighteen), a tube-drawer of 66 Conybere Street; Robert Barton (seventeen), a filer of 37 Charles Henry Street, and George Cosier (nineteen), a carter of 92 Barford Street.

But the only evidence the police had was that all of them were at the scene at the time of the tragedy, and were part of the fight which had taken place. As yet, the police had not had the time to ascertain which one had struck the fatal blow.

By March 1894 they had decided who that person was and at the Birmingham Assizes on Friday 16 March 1894 one man stood trial. This was John Thomas Cherry. The courtroom was crowded when Cherry took the stand and pleaded 'not guilty'.

The evidence showed that a fight between two gangs had erupted outside the museum vaults. John Cherry was in one gang; John Metcalf belonged to the other. Buckled belts and kicking were used. Then a knife was produced and witnesses said they definitely saw Cherry approach Metcalf. William Bond said Cherry slashed at him in the face with a knife, but, due to the numbers involved, there were many conflicting stories.

Like many old streets in Birmingham, Barford Street is now an industrial estate. (© V. Morgan)

However, it was revealed that Cherry had spoken openly about his involvement in the fight, but told William Berry that he didn't think he had done it because his knife wasn't in a good enough condition, although he did have it in his hand at the time.

Another acquaintance, William Craven, asked Cherry if he had been there. 'I was there but I don't know what I did. I was drunk. They all say I did it,' was the answer. Then Cherry showed him the knife. It had a white handle and a 3½-inch blade, but when arrested, the knife Cherry had said was his had a brown handle and a damaged blade. Police thought he had made a point of telling his friends he couldn't have done it because the blade was broken, and then swapped knives to cover his story.

Gradually the evidence became clearer. William Palmer said that Metcalf had been a member of the Park Street gang and Cherry was a member of the Barford Street gang. Another member of the Park Street gang, William Bond, had argued with William Fallon, a member of the Barford Street gang, and had gone out that night to tackle him.

Both gangs met nightly at the Museum Concert Hall. Bond, who was considered 'one of the commanding officers', had taken Palmer with him to stand guard at the door while he and Metcalf looked for Fallon. When Fallon came out, Metcalf knocked him down and the fight began.

George Edgar Dunn at first said that he had seen Cherry with a knife, but didn't see him do the stabbing. But after questioning he changed his mind and said it was definitely Cherry who had stabbed Metcalf. When Detective Squires arrested Cherry he insisted he was not guilty. Now, when Dunn had identified him, he said he was being set-up.

Throughout his trial Cherry had maintained a calm exposure, but he had eventually broken down when the witnesses for the defence were called. He sobbed with his head in his hands as Joseph Henry Skidmore, the barber who he had worked for three years, and his old headmaster, George William Davies, both described him as a quiet, well-behaved lad.

His defence counsel, Mr Dorsett, reminded the jury of the conflicting statements and of the unreliable witnesses, but Cherry was still found guilty.

The judge, Mr Baron Pollock, commented on the existence of gangs of roughs and the brutality in using belts and kicking people who were down on the ground. He said he would have had difficulty in being lenient with the prisoner, except that it appeared the attack was made in the heat of the moment and, due to his youth, Cherry may not have realised that the cut he was making would cause the death of someone. He sentenced Cherry to five years' penal servitude. The *Birmingham Daily Post* recorded that, 'The prisoner smiled, turned round, looked up at the gallery and laughed, and, with a wave of his hand, tripped gaily from the dock.'

The Murder of Quaint Mary

1898

Suspect:	*Claude Felix Mumby and James Twitty*
Age:	*Unknown*
Charge:	*Murder*
Sentence:	*Execution, later reduced to life imprisonment*

Mary Ann Alibon was sixty years old and lived along Latimer Street in Birmingham. She was born on 27 January 1839, the daughter of Joseph and Eleanor Alibon. Her parents must have either moved into Birmingham looking for work before they met, like so many young people at that time, or with their parents and siblings, as the census shows that Joseph was born in Pillerton Warwickshire around 1795, and Eleanor in Smethwick, Staffordshire around 1806. Mary had had a younger brother and sister, but they had died as children, so she became her parents only child. She never married.

On the 1841 and 1851 census Joseph was listed as a labourer in Tonks Street, but by the time of the 1861 census the family had moved to Thorpe Street and Joseph was a husker – a person who sells wares on the street, like a market trader, or sometimes may have had a small shop.

Joseph must have been successful as Mary inherited several small houses and a shop after both her mother and father had died. The shop was at 43 Thorpe Street and had been kept by her mother, Eleanor, after Joseph had died in 1868. Eleanor had died in 1884.

Thorpe Street. (© V. Morgan)

The undermentioned Houses are situate within the Boundaries of the

44 [Page 41]

No. of Schedule	ROAD, STREET, &c., and No. or NAME of HOUSE	HOUSES	NAME and Surname of each Person	RELATION to Head of Family	CON- DITION as to Marriage	AGE last Birthday of Males / Females	Rank, Profession, or OCCUPATION	WHERE BORN	If (1) Deaf-and-Dumb (2) Blind (3) Imbecile or Idiot (4) Lunatic
			Elizabeth Spurgeon	Gra. dau.		13	Scholar	Hertford Hereford	
			Christopher Heins	Son		6	Do	Warwick B'ham	
			Frederick do	Son		3	Do	Do do	
2/2	42 Trah St	1	Eleanor Alibon	Head		72		Staff Smethwick	
			Mary do	Dau.	Unm	42	Huckster	Warwick B'ham	
2/3	43 do	1	Benjamin Walker	Head	Mar	59	Master Gardener	Staff Tipton	
			Ann do	Wife	Mar	59		Do Wilnecote	
			William Smith	Boarder	Unm		Brickmakers Labourer	Warwick Cardington	
2/4	44 do	1	Thomas H Smith	Head	Mar		Brass Chandelier Merchant	Staff	
			Martha E Smith	Wife	Mar	47		Staff Sea and water	
			Ellen do	Dau.	Unm	17	Mill boy maker	Warwick B'ham	
			Minnie E do	Dau.			Scholar	Devon Exeter	
			Ada E do	Dau.		11	do	do do	
			Thomas H do	Son		8	do	Warwick B'ham	
			Emily B do	Dau.		6	do	do do	
			Mary Ann do	Dau.		3	do	do do	
			David E do	Son		1		do do	
2/5	45 do	1	George Foxham	Head	Mar		Pauper	do do	
			Ann do	Wife	Mar	53		Herts Brompore	
			Laura do	Dau.	Unm	26	Blister Maker	Warwick B'ham	
			George do	Son	Unm		Gun maker	do do	
			Ann do	Dau.	Unm	22		do do	
			Walter do	Son			Harmonium Maker	do do	
			John do	Son		13	Scholar	do do	

Total of Houses... 4   Total of Males and Females... 11 / 5

The 1881 census entry for Mary Alibon.
(RG11/2973/44/41. Held in Birmingham Archives and Heritage)

After her mother died Mary lived alone. She moved into one of her houses in Latimer Street where she became known for her eccentric habits. She always refused to have anyone to stay with her and did not even allow her relations to enter the house. Mary could have been described as quaint, but the newspapers of 1898 portrayed her as a lunatic and told how, seven years earlier, she had been a patient in Winson Green Asylum for eighteen weeks.

She suffered from delusions and often told people she was engaged to a colonel in the Volunteers. She had even had her wedding trousseau prepared and she would hire a cab, saying she was going to stay with him for a few days. Her relations would go and find her and bring her back home.

Her door was always locked and the milkman had to serve her through a window; the coal was delivered that way too. When she left the house she would climb through that same window, and then pay children to sit on her doorstep to guard the house until she came back.

She must have been wealthy as she had a telephone, and used it, she said, to talk to her dead mother.

Although eccentric, she was quite capable of collecting her rents which amounted to 32s per week. She employed two boys to make the rounds with her – one carried a satchel and one a carpet bag which, supposedly, held all her savings. Neighbours and passers-by would frequently hear her counting her money through her windows.

On the morning of 20 October 1898, two youths were seen leaving her house. It was assumed she'd employed them to carry her bags, but a few hours later it was noticed

Spring Hill Bridge. (© V. Morgan)

her door was ajar and the shutters were still closed. It was soon realised that nobody had been seen or heard anything of Mary that day and the police were called.

Police Constable Walters entered the house and searched the downstairs' rooms. Everything looked in order but there was no sign of Mary. When he went upstairs he found Mary's body on the bed with her hands tied to the bedposts with handkerchiefs, a handkerchief in her mouth and a piece of linen wrapped loosely around her neck. She had bruises on her face. The handkerchiefs were described as being the type labouring men used, and the linen around her neck had been torn from a garment stored in a box near the bed.

The surgeon said the linen around her neck had not been tight enough to kill her; it was the handkerchief in her mouth and her false teeth stuck down her throat which had caused her death.

A neighbour at 115 Latimer Street, whom newspapers described as the 'peaky-blinder' type, described one of the youths that had been seen: he had worn a dirty brown cap, a soiled brown coat and brown corduroy trousers.

Meanwhile, a young man by the name of Frank Jones had checked into a boarding house in West Bromwich. He had arrived between ten and eleven in the morning and seemed agitated. When asked if there was a problem he said he had walked from Birmingham and was tired and hungry. He was given ham and eggs for breakfast then went to his room. Later in the day, around five o'clock, he asked if the evening newspaper had come in. On buying one he opened it and quickly closed it again. At seven o'clock he bought another and took it to bed with him.

The next day the proprietor of the lodging house saw a description of the two youths in the newspaper. One fitted the description of the young man staying at his house – sallow complexion, short dark moustache and the beginnings of a beard on his chin. He sent for the police.

When arrested, Frank said he had been tramping the country and had been walking around Birmingham all night, so had probably been in Latimer Street. When searched he was found to have nearly a sovereign in silver coins. These, he said, were change from a sovereign he had found in the street. He had used it to buy some cigarettes on his way from Birmingham. But these coins matched the discoloured coins that had been left in Mary's house, money that hadn't been discovered by the assailants and was all hidden in a biscuit tin, an old tobacco box, a mustard tin and a cocoa tin. Mary also had a Post Office Savings book showing a balance of £31 10s.

Frank's real name was Claude Felix Mumby and he had once lived in Latimer Street. A youth named William Sullivan said he had heard Claude once say that he would like to get his hands on Mary's money. The night before the murder he had slept in the Erdington Workhouse.

At the inquest on Saturday 5 November he was found guilty of wilful murder and taken to Winson Green Gaol. Here he made a statement: 'The jury have found me guilty. I am now going to tell you the truth. The man that was with me I don't know his name; he gave the name of George at the Erdington Workhouse.'

All he claimed to know of this George was that he worked for a lame man in Aberystwyth, selling coal on a bag wagon; that his father, mother and brother also sold coal there, and that he had just come from Lichfield and was on his way to Bromsgrove.

They had waited outside Mary's house until half past midnight, then got into the cellar through the grating and sat on the steps until seven in the morning. When they went upstairs Mary was asleep and George wanted to 'do her in' but Claude had said, 'No, don't touch her.' Then she woke and when she saw them started screaming. They took hold of her and pushed George's handkerchief into her mouth to stop her. When they left, Claude said he thought she looked alright. 'I am sorry we done it,' he added. 'I never intended to kill her. We only had eighteen shillings each. The other chap left me on Spring Hill Bridge. He came back to town and I went to West Bromwich.'

A description of George was circulated and the master of the Merthyr Tydfil Workhouse recognised it. James Twitty was arrested on 20 November and brought back to Birmingham.

When Claude and James met again it was at the Birmingham Assizes. The jury found them both guilty of murder and the judge sentenced them to death. However, an appeal changed the verdict to manslaughter and they were both sentenced to life imprisonment.

In the 1901 census, they are both in prison in Tavistock, Devon, but by 1911 Claude was in a prison in Weymouth and James in Parkhurst on the Isle of Wight.

Claude died in 1921, aged forty-five, and James in 1948, aged seventy-three.

'I will kill him before the night is out!'

1912

Suspect:	John Edwards
Age:	Unknown
Charge:	Murder
Sentence:	Acquitted

By the early twentieth century the old back-to-back courts of Birmingham were showing their age and were described as squalid – more like slums than the comfortable cheap dwellings they had originally meant to be. Many of the individual homes in these courts still didn't have their own water supply, they were ill-lit, and a

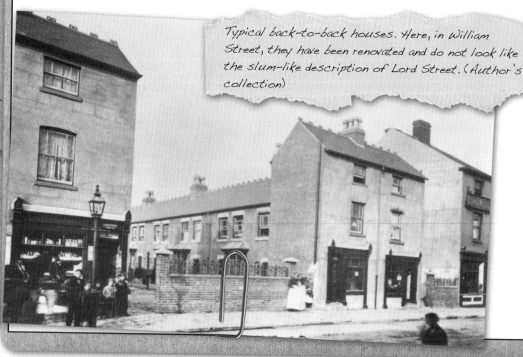

Typical back-to-back houses. Here, in William Street, they have been renovated and do not look like the slum-like description of Lord Street. (Author's collection)

lot still had the original privies. So it was little wonder that the people who lived in these courts weren't always happy, and the life they were forced to live often result in fights and arguments between neighbours.

One of these particular dwellings in Lord Street, described as a dingy court between small tenements, became the scene of a violent quarrel between neighbours and which ended in the fatal stabbing on one of its residents.

In 1911, the Pugh family were living in nearby Cromwell Street, at number 74. The family consisted of William Pugh and his wife of twenty-nine years, (Mary) Jane, and their six surviving children, ranging in age from two to seventeen. William earned a living as a stoker at the gas works.

At some time during the next twelve months, William and Jane Pugh made the fatal decision to move a short distance away, to the back of 83 Lord Street. Here, at the back of 88 Lord Street, lived twenty-two-year-old Florence Williams and her lodger, twenty-nine-year-old John Edwards. William and Jane's eldest son, also called William, had known John Edwards for about two or three years, but Edwards had only lived with Florence for a few months.

On the night of Sunday, 5 May 1912, at around ten o'clock, there was a knock on the door of the Pugh's house. William Snr got up to answer it and found a neighbour, Mr Broomhall, standing there, and they stood talking for a short while. During this time, John Edwards and another neighbour came up to William and challenged him to a fight.

Pugh's son, William Jnr, had been upstairs when he heard the disturbance down in the yard. He heard John Edwards say, 'There's only one man I have a grudge against in this yard and I will kill him before the night is out! And that's Pughie.' William Jnr rushed downstairs to find his father taking his coat off out in the yard. Edwards was already in his shirtsleeves and calling for his brother Bill and Florence to fetch two pokers.

Either someone called the police, or they had heard the commotion as they passed the entrance to the court, but officers arrived and ordered everyone to go back into their houses. Everything went quiet – but not for long.

A short time later there was a loud knocking on the Pugh's door. It was John Edwards who called out, 'I have got a brother who will fight your son for a pound.' Jane begged her husband to ignore it, but when Edwards began kicking at the door, their son William went out and a fight ensued between him and Edwards' brother, Bill. William Pugh Snr stood watching from the door as a small crowd gathered.

Edwards was seen to creep around the crowd towards William Pugh Snr and then appear to punch him in the chest saying, 'There's one for you. I told you I'd do it on you.'

At the same time, William Pugh Jnr, while still fighting, slipped and fell in the gutter. As he was getting up he heard his father say, 'I'm stabbed,' and saw Edwards draw something shiny from the right side of his father's chest. William Snr fell into his wife's arms and blood began to seep through his shirt. William Jnr ran to the telephone box to call for help.

Birmingham General Hospital, built in 1897, on the corner of Steelhouse Lane and Loveday Street. (Author's collection)

William Pugh was taken to the hospital in a horse ambulance, but he had lost a lot of blood and doctors had no hope of him recovering. He was given treatment in the casualty department first and then sent up to a ward, where he died half an hour later.

Police Inspector Street had been passing close to the court at the time of the fight and had heard someone calling him, shouting, 'Make haste, someone's been stabbed.' He arrived in the court just as they were taking William Pugh away. Mrs Pugh pointed to William Edwards and said it was him who had stabbed her husband. He was immediately arrested, but several people said she was wrong and so he was released.

At the hospital, William Pugh managed to tell police that, 'it was the tall man that did it.' His wife then changed her statement, saying it must have been the brother. 'They're very much alike. I can't tell them apart.' Her son, William, also said it was John Edwards he had seen. So the police returned to the court to arrest John Edwards and make further enquiries.

No one really seemed to know, or want to say, exactly what had happened. The neighbours were caught between the two sides. Jane Pugh and Florence Williams had often had arguments over the children. Some said there was a long-standing hatred between several of the residents, especially the women, and that there was a grudge between Jane's husband, William, and Florence's lodger, John Edwards. There had even been some talk that day that Edwards had intended to kill Pugh sometime that night. When everyone was later saying that no one knew who had done it, Florence had said, 'Isn't there? There's one who knows.'

Ethel Broomhall said she saw Florence pass something bright to Edwards. And William Humpage, looking down from his window at 90 Lord Street, said he saw Florence go into her house and return with something bright in her hand. She then crossed the yard to Pugh's door. Humpage said he had shouted, 'Look out, she's got a knife!'

When asked about a knife, Florence fetched a shovel handle and said that was what she had.

Edwards' sister, Lucy Higgins, said it was Florence who had actually done it. She had, on other occasions, seen Florence strike Pugh several times after he had insulted her. But she did admit to being drunk at the time of this recent attack.

On being arrested, Edwards said, 'I have plenty of witnesses. I did not come home till half past ten.' Later, he said he had been in the house when Pugh had been taken to hospital, so hadn't known anything about it. He claimed he had looked out and seen about seven or eight men in the yard at the time, so it could have been any one of them.

Florence Williams was arrested as being an accessory.

There now followed a number of hearings before the magistrates in order to determine exactly what did happen. These were spread over the course of about three weeks; by now murder cases were becoming more as we know them today – no quick arrest, followed by a court appearance then a sentence.

There already appeared to be doubt in the magistrate's mind, as he asked whether there was anything to connect the prisoner with the crime. Superintendent Shakespeare said he had five witnesses, though their evidence was 'shifting a bit', but they had one witness who had said they had seen the prisoner take his hand away from Pugh's chest.

The hearing was adjourned while more investigations were made. By the next hearing, on the 15 May, the police had found the bloodstained knife in an outbuilding in the court. The prosecutor, Mr J.E. Hill, asked if the hearing could again be adjourned to allow time for the analyst to complete his report, and an adjournment was granted until the following Tuesday.

When the inquest was finally concluded it only took the jury twenty minutes to find a verdict of insufficient evidence. The judge was forced to release the suspects and commented that he had never heard such a mass of contradictions in his life.

UNSOLVED

'I have given you the opportunity'

1912

Suspect:	George Wake
Age:	Unkown
Charge:	Arson with attempt to defraud
Sentence:	Acquitted

At two o'clock on the morning of 24 August 1912, an explosion was heard at a motor and coach garage owned by George Wake. By the time the fire brigade arrived at the scene, there was a furious blaze raging in the storeroom in a remote part of the building. They tried to put the fire out but the water didn't seem to be working.

Denis Motor fire engine, c. 1911. (Author's collection)

The Old Square and the Priory area. (© V. Morgan)

They then found tins of calcium carbide near the door of the room; but throwing water onto this simply fed the fire. There were also tins of paraffin, turpentine and lubricating oil.

Suspicion surrounded the fire: the Northern Insurance Company stated that the claim which followed appeared higher than was estimated. Mr F. Sharp, George Wake's accountant, said the books were showing a deficiency of £4,318 and there was an overdraft at the bank for £1,528, and that prior to the blaze the police had already been told that Wake had discussed setting fire to the buildings for insurance purposes. In fact, they had been watching the premises and a constable had seen the manager enter the property at an unusual hour, then leave six minutes later, just prior to the explosion.

George Wake had originally kept a public house. Then, in about 1899, he had started buying land and building houses. Wake now owned about 250 furnished houses and shops in Birmingham, and earned a weekly rent of between £50 and £70. He had bought his garage at Priory Exchange, Upper Priory, in March 1910.

In May 1912, George Wake had gone round to collect his rent from his tenants. One was Leonard Wilkinson, who had spent five years in prison after stealing a letter containing a cheque for £250. Wake asked Leonard if he would like to manage his garage at the Priory Exchange, off the Old Square, but Leonard was not keen as he had heard business was very bad. George convinced him business was picking up and that Leonard would receive a good commission, so Leonard accepted the offer.

Two months later business still hadn't picked up and, when George Wake came around demanding his rent, Leonard was unable to pay. George said he would give him a little longer, but said if he didn't pay he would turn him out and take the furniture back.

George then had an idea and told Leonard that he had done pretty well out of a fire he had had at a house in Bearwood, so thought they could have a fire at the Priory. Leonard protested but Wake said he wasn't asking him to do it as he would get a member of his family to do it. All he wanted Leonard to do was order a large amount of stock. These goods would then be stored at his house and he would put old stuff in the garage. Leonard was also to prepare a stock book. George said Leonard would have something out of it, depending on what was received from the insurance company, but Leonard was adamant that he didn't want to be involved.

George was back again at the beginning of August asking for his rent, which Leonard still couldn't pay.

'I have given you the opportunity to earn the money,' George reminded him.

Still Leonard refused, and again George said he would turn him out of both his house and his job and make sure no one else hired him.

'We need not have a very big one as the water would spoil a lot of stock,' George had said, and reminded Leonard that he would get a member of the family to do the deed. All he needed to do was enter all the stock in the books. This time Leonard agreed.

Empty drums were entered in the books as being filled with white lead, and empty tins of oil as being full. Twelve dozen sash tools were listed, when there were actually only four dozen, and seven very old cart horse collars were entered as practically new. Motor wheels, which had originally cost £2 10s, were entered as £18. The total value added up to £1,600. But Wake said it wasn't enough. He bought more goods and had them entered at inflated prices.

Frank Fairfield Norris was the secretary of the company and was also an ex-convict. He had served five years for falsifying accounts – it seemed George liked to surround himself with villains and Frank was also pulled into George's plan. However, Frank went away to London on the night of the crime so he would not be implicated.

He was asked by George what they were insured for and whether it included third party risk. Frank had said yes, then heard Leonard say, 'I shall see that there is no petrol on the premises,' but Frank noticed that there was more oil in the shop than normal. He was then told to enter in the stock book; a settee for £15, a suit for £9, a vacuum cleaner for £16 and a governess car head for £10. Then he heard Leonard being told to enter forty motor wheels at between 8s and 9s each, and a number of motor wings at 5s to 6s each, although twenty-six had been purchased at £2 10s and had been in stock for some time – ten had already been sold. The conversation also included the four-seat motor car being left upstairs, and for three dozen dandy brushes to be entered in the book, even though there were only ever a dozen at a time on the premises.

'They won't be able to tell how many,' George had commented.

Wake was going on holiday on 14 August to Ostend, so wanted the fire to take place then; he had also been away on the Isle of Man when the Bearwood fire had taken place.

Then, the night before, he told Leonard he couldn't get anyone to do it, 'You will have to see to it yourself.' Leonard was told to start the fire by the storeroom door and to leave the door open in order to cause a draught.

On 7 September, Leonard was discharged from the Police Court in order to give evidence for the prosecution. The case lasted throughout September and into October, over eleven days. George Wake's defence lawyer, Hugo Young, said the only evidence implicating him was on the statements of his two employees, both of whom had served penal servitude – Wilkinson for an 'offence of great craftiness' who, when caught, had accused someone else.

The other witness was David Jackson, who was no longer on friendly terms with Wake. They had originally met at an auction. Early in 1911, Wake had had the idea of turning his business into a company, in order to get credit. Wake's solicitor had advised him to form a limited company, rather than a partnership with Jackson, so if Jackson did anything, the lawsuit would be against the company and not Wake himself. But after Jackson had agreed to become a partner, he claimed that Wake's attitude towards him had changed – he acted as 'master over me and everyone,' and used bad language.

Jackson had been the acting manager for twelve months when the idea of a fire was first suggested. Wake had said, 'We can get plenty of credit and stuff the place full of goods and have a jolly good fire.' Jackson had refused to be involved. Wake had said, 'I will have a fire on my own if you won't.' Jackson also said he had warned Wake that Norris had been convicted when he was hired, but Wake had said, 'He may be useful to us for some other purpose.'

Wake had fired Jackson for using the garage for betting purposes and when he had taken Wake to court for unfair dismissal he had lost and ended up bankrupt. It had been David Jackson who had informed the police there might be a fire.

George Wake was sent for trial at the assizes, charged with setting fire to the premises of the Priory Exchange with the intent to defraud, and with inciting Leonard Wilkinson to set fire to the premises with intent to defraud. At the assizes on December 14th, Hugo Young accused Wilkinson of telling lies in order to save his own neck. He suggested that perhaps Wilkinson had sold stock improperly and thought a fire would make it difficult to discover. When called to give evidence, even Norris tried to turn the tables, saying that he only knew of the intention to set fire to the premises from Wilkinson, not from Wake himself.

Mr Justice Scrutten addressed the jury and advised them not to convict on the testimony of Wilkinson or Norris unless they felt it corroborated with some other evidence. He reminded them that Jackson was 'brimming over with spite', so should be ignored. He asked them to consider if the fire was started out of spite, or as a cover-up for any inappropriate dealings with Wake's stock and money. Had Wilkinson and Norris been robbing their employer and trying to cover their tracks. Or was, indeed, the prisoner guilty?

The jury decided George Wake was not guilty.

UNSOLVED

If you enjoyed this book, you may also be interested in …

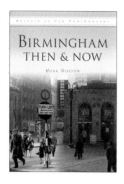

Birmingham Then & Now
MARK NORTON

Take a nostalgic visual journey back to 1960s Birmingham to witness the much-loved Bull Ring, the grand city-centre buildings that were demolished to make way for the 'modern' city, and the streets and courts that were swept away during the last fifty years of development. Mark Norton presents many previously unpublished pictures alongside his own colour photographs of the area in the twenty-first century. Detailed captions provide a new insight into the ever-changing city.

978 0 7524 5722 2

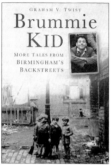

Brummie Kid: More Tales from Birmingham's Backstreets
GRAHAM V. TWIST

Brummie Kid is a fascinating recollection of the experience of growing up in the slums of Nechells and Aston. Despite hard living conditions and a distinct lack of money, a strong community spirit prevailed and families and neighbourhoods were close-knit. In these tough times you hoped nobody noticed you going to the 'pop shop' to pawn precious valuables, siphoning petrol from cars under the nose of the local bobby, or sneaking into the flicks without paying – though everyone was more or less in the same boat.

978 0 7524 5391 0

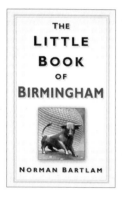

The Little Book of Birmingham
NORMAN BARTLAM

The Little Book of Birmingham is a funny, fast-paced, fact-packed compendium of the sort of frivolous, fantastic or simply strange information which no one will want to be without. Here we find out about the city's most unusual crimes and punishments, eccentric inhabitants, famous sons and daughters and literally hundreds of wacky facts. A reference book and a quirky guide, this can be dipped in to time and time again to reveal something you never knew.

978 0 7524 6349 0

Birmingham: A History in Maps
PAUL LESLIE LINE

From the town plans and maps contained within this unique volume emerges a social picture of Birmingham; a town quickly growing in size and population in the eighteenth century. Land was bought up for development and hundreds of 'courts' were built to home the industrial workers pouring in from the outlying villages. Accompanied with informative text and pictures of the cityscape, this book is a must for all local historians.

978 0 7524 5281 4

Visit our website and discover thousands of other History Press books.

www.thehistorypress.co.uk